The Eternal
Path of Charity

Al Fatihah: The Opening

In the name of Allah, the Most Gracious, the Most Merciful.

All praise and thanks are Allah's, the Lord of mankind, jinn and all that exists;

The Most Gracious, the Most Merciful;

The only Owner (and the only Ruling Judge) of the day of recompense;

You (Alone) we worship, and You (Alone) do we ask for help.

Guide us to the Straight Path;

The Way of those on whom You have bestowed Your Grace;

Not (the way) of those who earned Your anger, nor of those who You sent astray.

(Quran; 1:1-7)

"Invite mankind to the way of Your Lord with wisdom and fair preaching and argue with them in the way that is best. Truly your Lord knows best who has gone astray from His Path and He is Best Knower of those who are guided "

(Quran; 16:125)

The Eternal
Path of Charity

Zin Eddine Dadach

MV Publishers

Published by MV Publishers, a subsidiary of Muslim Voice, 12719 Hillmeade Station Dr, Bowie, MD 20720, USA. MVPublishers@muslimvoice.org

ISBN 978-1-956601-03-9

First edition 2022
Printed in the United States of America

Zin Eddine Dadach, 1957–
The Eternal Path of Charity / Zin Eddine Dadach

ISBN 978-1-956601-03-9

To My Father "The Happy Fisherman"

At the end of July of 1980, my parents organized a family gathering to celebrate my departure to New York City (USA) to start my graduate studies. The night before, my father went fishing and came back early morning in a happy mood with some fish in his hands and few stories to tell. My mother cleaned up the fish and prepared an oven baked fish and vegetables for dinner, which is my father's favorite dish. During a lively discussion and questions about my new life in New York City, my parents seemed a little bit worried. By the end of the late dinner, we were having mint tea and my father came closer to me and said "We know how important people are to us only when they leave us".

Now that he has left this world, I know what he meant.

Contents

Foreword

In the Name of Allah, The Merciful

Praise Be to Allah (SWT), Lord of the Worlds, and may blessings and peace be upon our Prophet Muhammad, and those who follow him and are guided by him until the Day of Judgment.

This book inspired my admiration because the author dealt with the subject of charity in a new way that I had not previously known, in accordance with the methodology of Sharia and reasoning. His work is drawn from his graduate studies in the natural sciences, conducting lab experiments, his observations of a widely diverse group of people, and wider contemplations of the universe. The professor concludes that the universe is governed by charity, and its principle is based on the law of giving and receiving. This law of charity and its principle perpetuates life in the world of the living.

The honorable professor concluded that the scientific principles belong to a divine science imposed by Allah (SWT) on the whole universe, and that the universe is a universal school for humanity.

Our professor has also strived towards a clarification of the concept of charity and its impact on human life. He posits that charity entails achieving the reward of happiness from Allah (SWT), so by helping others, we will help ourselves. Charity is not limited to giving favor with financial contributions, but is broader, as it includes helping the distressed, kind words and any act of support towards others. To illustrate, prophet Mohammad (PBUH) said: "Charity is prescribed for every person every day the sun rises. To administer justice between two people is charity. To assist a man upon his mount so that he may ride it is charity. To place his luggage on the animal is charity. To remove harm from the road is charity. A good word is charity. Each step taken toward prayer is charity."[Al-Bukhari] [Muslim]

Charity is a moral value that dissolves selfishness in the human soul, just as heat melts the ice but its dimensions in the life of a non-Muslim are different from it in the life of a Muslim. The Western man or others rush to charity seeking the happiness of others. As for the Muslim, he rushes to it to please Allah (SWT) only. It brings happiness to its owner and to those who deserve it, and it brings closeness to Allah (SWT) and the steps to Paradise, and moves one further from Hell.

Thank you, sir, for this intellectual creativity, because the Islamic Library is in dire need of this kind of study that is used to invite people to the Straight Path of Allah (SWT).

Rajab 22, 1442 corresponding to 03/06/2021

Professor Nesreddine Ghezal.

Preface

"O mankind! We have created you from a male and a female, and made you into nations and tribes so that you may know one another" (Quran; 49:13)

Originally from Algeria, I studied in very different cities including New York City (USA), Quebec City (Canada) and Osaka (Japan). Due to my thirst for knowledge, I embarked on graduate studies to explore the unknown world and human nature. These living and educational experiences gave me the opportunity to learn about very different aspects of natural science by conducting experiments in laboratories, and also to further discover diverse facets of human nature by interacting with different cultures, religions and social backgrounds. With commitment to my Muslim heritage, my biggest challenge was to seek an understanding of differences between cultures and religions without losing my source. As if I were searching for something deep inside me, naively I removed my cultural slippers to feel the warmth and the coldness of human nature. Therefore, my curiosity pushed me to cross borders in order to explore cultural and religious practices in depth.

Initially, I noticed many similarities between human beings, since we often experience emotions for the same reasons. One of my best memories that proves that human beings have similar feelings is when some of my friends of different cultures found love and embarked on intercultural marriages. Moreover, while practices and conventions may differ, the underlying motivations and needs that unite human beings are the same. For example, some cultures use cutlery to eat, whereas others use their hands or chopsticks, but everyone is eating for sustenance and survival. Similarly, the need to communicate and express human feelings encompasses the use of many languages and dialects. The practices of faith also vary widely, which I noticed in detail from visiting churches in New York City and Quebec, and shrines in Japan, and observing religious practices in those cities.

At the end of my travels, with my mind full of so many exciting experiences, I went back to Algeria to rest, reflect and consider my future. During the first months in my hometown, I realized that the immersion in different cultures had caused changes within me and my thinking. Since I had the opportunity to discover myself through people with different backgrounds, I have come to see humanity as a tree with a single root, with each branch offering a different kind of fruit. As a consequence, I feel more attached to the invisible world than the cultural and physical aspects of our existence. In order to explore the impact of my travel experiences on my faith, I decided to deepen my knowledge in Islam by listening on a daily basis to resources, such as "Tafseer Al Quran" (explanation of Quran) and "Asma Allah Al Hosna" (The Beautiful Names of Allah (SWT) by Dr. Mohammed Rateb al-Nabulsi. I felt inner peace and joy knowing that the messages contained within resonated with lessons learnt from my travel experiences. In particular, the very fruitful and clear explanation given by Dr. Nabulsi about the importance of first knowing Allah (SWT), through His creation and signs in the universe in order to worship Him, as it should be. From this perspective, most Muslims know and practice the five pillars of Islam: The Profession of Faith (Shahada); Daily Prayers (Salat); Alms-Giving (Zakat); Fasting during Ramadan (Saum) and Pilgrimage to Mecca (Hajj). However, like any building or structure, these five pillars must have a foundation. According to my personal interpretation, this foundation is like the soul of Islam that makes our faith (Iman) in Allah (SWT) strong. The five pillars of Islam are the body parts that one must know in order to practice our faith with love and thankfulness. Notably, the three most important elements of the soul of Islam are:

Al-Eaql (Mind): This is an indispensable attribute of human beings; it is what distinguishes them from other creatures. No creature is blessed with the type of mind human beings have.

This is the most beautiful treasure from Allah (SWT) to humanity in order to guide us to perceive His signs around us.

Al-Fitrah (Goodness): Islam is the religion of Goodness because human beings are born to do good deeds, to be kind and to help others. Considering my travel experiences, I encountered good people everywhere. This confirms that Al Fitrah does not belong to any particular cultural or religious background.

Al Tawheed (Oneness of Allah (SWT)): Al Tawheed means that Allah (SWT) is One, without partner in His dominion and His actions. Al-Eaql and Al-Fitrah are the two paths to perceive the reality of Al Tawheed. Moreover, in order to help us adopt Al Tawheed in our daily actions, Allah (SWT) sent Prophets and books to guide humanity to worship Him alone.

In conclusion, my current knowledge and perception has led me to conclude that spirituality is needed in Islam in order to be able to perceive that Allah (SWT) alone governs everything behind the stage of the visible material world. For my part, I realize now that the hidden Hand of Allah (SWT) was guiding me through every event of my life, whether positive or negative. At times this has created beneficial opportunities in my life, and has also steered me away from potentially harmful situations or choices.

About the Book

If you ever have been fully engaged in any social or professional activity, you might have been experiencing a mental state that psychologists define as "flow". You are completely involved and you feel enjoyment in the process of the activity. Some might experience this pleasure while engaging in a sport and others might have such an experience while engaged in an activity such as painting, reading, or fishing. For some, this activity involves helping people, animals or plants in one way or another, which relates to the state of the soul introduced in this book called "The Eternal Path of Charity". Indeed, during any charity-based activity, you will feel some kind of tranquility in your heart and sometimes, you will even experience tears of inner joy. This means that you are putting the path of your life in the pleasant Eternal Path of Charity. It should be noted that the purpose of life for human beings and all creatures is to worship Allah (SWT) alone and helping others are the highest acts of worship.

> "See you not that whoever is in the heavens and whoever is on the earth, and the sun, and the moon, and the stars, and the mountains, and the trees, and living creatures, beasts and many of mankind prostate themselves to Allah ..."

(Quran; 22:18)

This Quranic verse aroused my curiosity in order to find the commonality in the commandments of Allah (SWT) related to the universe and human beings and encouraged me to write this book. My exploration is predominantly based on lessons learnt from professional experiences over the duration of my travels and the lectures of Dr. Mohammed Rateb al-Nabulsi. First, since I have been for many years conducting research in different types of scientific fields and utilized diverse theories to interpret data from my experiments, I realized that, if the mathematical models used in different fields of science look different in the application, they have a similar profound concept. I came to the conclusion that these scientific principles could belong to one divine science imposed by Allah (SWT) on the whole universe. This supposition informed my spirituality, and encouraged me to look for the hidden forces beyond the material world. Secondly, based on the lessons learned from the lectures of Dr. Nabulsi, I have come to the understanding that the soul of Islam is crucial to have a strong faith in order to worship Allah (SWT) with love and thankfulness. The adoration of Allah (SWT) in this book is related to adding our daily actions during social and professional activities as good deeds in the Eternal Path of Charity.

Beautiful Names of Allah (SWT)

"Have they not travelled through the land, and have they hearts wherewith to and understand and ears wherewith to hear? Verily, it is not the eyes that grow blind, but it is the hearts which are in the breasts that grow blind" (Quran; 22:46)

During a cloudy day of January of 1981, I went with my Algerian friend Ahmed to Midtown Manhattan in New York City to visit the Empire state building. Due to the bad weather, we met only a few visitors as we took the elevator to the 102th floor. From the top of the edifice, all the buildings of the city were hidden below the clouds but we were very surprised and excited to see the blue sky above us on this dark day. Just after leaving the edifice, it started to rain and we decided to take the bus and return to the hotel for international students called "International House". From the bus stop of Columbia University, as we decided to walk to enjoy the sounds and the smell of the heavy rain, we were very happy to see the sunshine again. I would say on reflection, after my life experience, that in order to perceive the sun during a cloudy day, I had to open the spiritual eyes of my heart. I conclude that the Light of Allah (SWT) is always here to guide us even if sometimes there is some cloudiness in our life.

> *"Allah: there is no true God but Him. The Ever-Living, the Divine Master of all. Neither drowsiness nor sleep overtakes Him. His is all that is in the heavens and all that is on earth. Who is there that can intercede with Him, except by His permission? He knows all that lies open before them and all that lies hidden from them; whereas they cannot attain to anything of His knowledge save as He wills. His throne extends over the heavens and the earth, and the preservation of both does not tire Him. He is the Most High, the Most Great." (Quran; 2:255)*

Allah (SWT) means The God in Arabic. The word is derived by contraction from Al-Ilāh. The words "El" and "Ellah" are also the Hebrew and Aramaic words for God[1]. The first pillar of faith in Islam is Belief in Him in order to worship Him with love, fear and trust. For this purpose, Allah (SWT) describes Himself to us through His Ninety-Nine Beautiful Names (Table 1) in the Noble Quran and the Prophet (PBUH)'s sayings. Therefore, learning about His Beautiful Names is knowing what we are created for, and to ignore their meaning would be to neglect what we are living for. In fact, the more we learn about the Beautiful Names of Allah (SWT), the more we increase our Muslim faith. There is therefore nothing more sacred and blessed than understanding the meaning of the Beautiful Names of Allah (SWT) and, most importantly, living by them. For example, as indicated in the Quranic verse "

> *Allah is the Creator of all things and He is the guardian of all things." (Quran; 39:62),*

the Beautiful Name **"The Creator"** means that Allah (SWT) created us and everything else in the universe. Moreover, based on the Quranic verse

> *"Allah, The Self-sufficient Master, whom all creatures need" (Quran; 112:2)*

the Beautiful Name **"The Satisfier of Needs"** means that He is the One who can satisfy each need in a way He knows is best, while He is without any need. He is the One upon who all of creation depends, while He depends on no one. Furthermore, according to the Noble Quran:

> *"Verily they are enemies to me except the Lord. Who has created me and it is He Who guides me. And it is He who feeds me and gives me to drink. And when I am ill, it is He who cures me." (Quran; 51:58),*

we should be very thankful to Allah (SWT) because He not only guides us through life with the Noble Quran and The Prophet (PBUH) but also provides everything to all living creatures. His provision is endless including all material things, like money, food, water, air, shelter, and protection. As well as meeting our physiological needs, He (SWT) also provides for our psychological needs. For example, He gives us love through the love of our parents. Moreover, we also enjoy beautiful flowers, cute animals, delicious food, tasty drinks, vegetables and fruits of different flavors, shapes and colors. And the only thing He asks in return is thanks for these blessings by showing love to Him and all His creatures.

"And He is with you (by His knowledge) wheresoever you may be" (Quran; 57:4)

The most sincere manifestation of Muslim faith is to live our life feeling that Allah (SWT) is always with us with His Beautiful Names. Therefore, if we do anything, He is **"The All-Seeing"**, if we say something, He is **"The All-Hearing"** and if we think about anything, He is **"The All-Knowing"**. As mentioned in Noble Quran

"So, whosoever does good equal to the weight of an atom (or a small ant) shall see it. And whosoever does evil equal to the

weight of an atom (or a small ant) shall see it"
(Quran; 99:7-8),

this feeling of His presence scares the believers and helps them stay away from bad deeds because He is **"The Reckoner"**. Finally, as mentioned in the Quranic verse

"They have no protector other than Him, and He makes none to share in His Decision and His rule" (Quran; 18:26),

we should worship Him alone because He is the **"The Protecting Associate"** of the believers.

As a consequence, knowing the meaning of the Beautiful Names of Allah (SWT) allows us to thank Him for all that He has provided to make our life comfortable, to trust Him (Tawakkul) when we need help to solve our daily problems and therefore fulfill our divine duties with love and thankfulness. On a last note, Prophet Muhammad (PBUH) said: "Allah has Ninety-Nine Beautiful Names and whoever knows their meaning will enter to Paradise"[2].

Table 1: The Beautiful Names of Allah (SWT)[3]

Entirely Merciful	The Bestower of Mercy	The King and Owner of Dominion	The Absolutely Pure
The Perfection and Giver of Peace	The One Who gives Emaan and Security	The Guardian, The Witness, The Overseer	The All Mighty
The Compeller, The Restorer	The Supreme, The Majestic	The Creator, The Maker	The Originator
The Fashioner	The All- and Oft-Forgiving	The Subduer, The Ever-Dominating	The Giver of Gifts
The Provider	The Opener, The Judge	The All-Knowing, The Omniscient	The Withholder
The Extender	The Reducer, The Abaser	The Exalter, The Elevator	The Honourer, The Bestower
The Dishonourer, The Humiliator	The All-Hearing	The All-Seeing	The Judge, The Giver of Justice
The Utterly Just	The Subtle One, The Most Gentle	The Acquainted, the All-Aware	The Most Forbearing
The Magnificent, The Supreme	The Forgiving, The Exceedingly Forgiving	The Most Appreciative	The Most High, The Exalted

The Greatest, The Most Grand	The Preserver, The All-Heedful and All-Protecting	The Sustainer	The Reckoner, The Sufficient
The Majestic	The Most Generous, The Most Esteemed	The Watchful	The Responsive One
The All-Encompassing, the Boundless	The All-Wise	The Most Loving	The Glorious, The Most Honorable
The Resurrector, The Raiser of the Dead	The All- and Ever Witnessing	The Absolute Truth	The Trustee, The Disposer of Affairs
The All-Strong	The Firm, The Steadfast	The Protecting Associate	The Praiseworthy
The All-Enumerating, The Counter	The Originator, The Initiator	The Restorer, The Reinstater	The Giver of Life
The Bringer of Death, the Destroyer	The Ever-Living	The Sustainer, The Self-Subsisting	The Perceiver
The Illustrious, the Magnificent	The One	The Unique, The Only One	The Eternal, Satisfier of Needs
The Capable, The Powerful	The Omnipotent	The Expediter, The Promoter	The Delayer, the Retarder

The First	The Last	The Manifest	The Hidden One, Knower of the Hidden
The Governor, The Patron	The Self Exalted	The Source of Goodness, the Kind Benefactor	The Ever-Pardoning, The Relenting
The Avenger	The Pardoner	The Most Kind	Master of the Kingdom, Owner of the Dominion
Possessor of Glory and Honour, Lord of Majesty and Generosity	The Equitable, the Requiter	The Gatherer, the Uniter	The Self-Sufficient, The Wealthy
The Enricher	The Withholder	The Distresser	The Propitious, the Benefactor
The Light, The Illuminator	The Guide	The Incomparable Originator	The Ever-Surviving, The Everlasting
The Inheritor, The Heir	The Guide, Infallible Teacher	The Forbearing, The Patient	

Charity: The Divine Science

"So Exalted is Allah, the True King. None has the right to be worshipped but Him. The Lord of the Supreme Throne."
(Quran; 23:116)

Arriving in Japan in November of 1994, I learned that the Japanese celebrate every New Year as the new beginning of life. People clean up their homes, buy expensive gifts to renew their relationships and shrines and temples become crowded. On January 1st of 1995, I took this opportunity to visit one of the shrines of Ikeda city where I used to live. The smell of incense was everywhere, and I was curiously watching people ringing a large bell one after the other with a rope. After this ritual, they all bowed and clapped their hands twice. While taking pictures around the shrine, a priest invited me to go inside to visit the place. As we walked slowly through the rooms, he explained the history of the shrine. After about an hour, he accompanied me to the outside door and bowed and said "Shitsureishimashita (Sorry I disturbed you)". I was humbled because in actual fact it was me who disturbed him but, at the same time, I knew that Japanese people show respect to others by bowing. For example, Saikeirei is the most formal bow and takes the longest time. It is usually used to express deference to people of a very high social status. From this enriching experience of a Japanese religion, I reflected on the following: Since Allah (SWT) is "The King and Owner of Dominion", we are all supposed to bow to glorify Him and accept every single one of His orders with love and thankfulness. In reality, everything in this universe, such as the plants, animals and planets, are bowing to Allah (SWT) because they are accepting to fulfill the purpose for which He created them. Therefore, the whole universe is Muslim since it is in a state of obeisance to Allah (SWT)[4].

"It is He Who created the night and the day, and the sun and the moon. Each of them is floating in its orbit."
(Quran; 21:33)

Considering His beautiful Name "The Originator", Allah (SWT) designed the universe as a dynamic and organized system where all the components move in a highly planned way. For example, earth, which is the third planet from the sun, continuously rotates over twenty-four hours. According to this rotation, we have days and nights on earth, we have daylight for the part of earth that is facing the sun and it is dark for the other part of earth. We usually know the time of day by the position of the sun in the sky. Most people take roads and highways at sunrise for their daily social and professional activities and return home at sunset for family time and rest. While rotating, the earth also orbits the sun in three hundred and sixty-five days. As mentioned in the two Quranic verses "Verily, the number of months with Allah is twelve months (in a lunar year) so it was ordained by Allah on the day when He created the heavens and the earth" (Quran; 9:36) and "It is He Who made the sun a shining thing and the moon as a light and measured out for in stages that you might know the number of years and the reckoning."(Quran; 10:5), there are twelve months in one lunar year and we can count days, weeks, months and years with the size of the crescent and the moon.

> "And they think deeply about the creation of the heavens and the earth, (saying): Our Lord! You have not created (all) this without purpose. Glory to You!" (Quran; 3:191)

It seems like Allah (SWT) created the universe as a global school for humanity in order to contemplate it to perceive His lessons and thank Him for all His Favors. For example, through the change of nature over the four seasons, Allah (SWT) teaches us several lessons and reminds us of His Blessings. Indeed, the transformation of the weather during the four seasons shows how Allah (SWT) has coordinated the rotations of earth, the moon and the sun in order to make our life change through variations of feelings to avoid boredom. My best memories of this beautiful harmony between the variation of the weather and people's behavior and mood was in Quebec City (Canada).

Starting from the summer of 1991, I will never forget going to the old town called "Vieux Quebec" and walking through the narrow and animated streets full of Quebeckers and tourists wearing colorful shirts and short pants. The sunshine and the warm weather put everyone in a joyful mood and the lively discussions of people having ice cream under the sun, the smiling clowns and the beats of rhythmic music made the atmosphere even happier. I still remember those evenings where various international music events were organized in different parks of the city and many spectators sang until dawn. It seemed to me like a recreation time after the long and cold winter as a gift from Allah (SWT).

After this brief and lovely summer of beauty and relaxation, the autumn of 1991 was another palette of colors but a cooler season. A light rain began to fall and the green leaves in the different parks of the city started to turn slowly to the autumn colors yellow, orange and brown. This progressive adjustment during autumn teaches us that any change in our life should also be done gradually. During that beautiful season called "The Indian summer", many people were enjoying sunshine and the beautiful colors of autumn were everywhere. I still remember sitting down for hours inside the parks of Laval University to contemplate the arranged rows of multicolored trees. I also visited the "Vieux Quebec" with some international students to enjoy the unusually warm weather around the famous hotel "Château Frontenac". We walked through the very popular and narrow street called "Rue Du Trésor" where local painters display their drawings on the walls for sale. By the end of October, the trees of the city started losing slowly their leaves and some people were collecting them near their homes in orange bags that reminded me of Halloween. As the buses started to be quieter, I was surprised to see some people were impatient waiting for the first snowstorm of the long and cold winter. I realized later that winter in Quebec City is not only a season but also part of their cultural heritage.

When a northern wind began to blow, we had the first snow. The days became much shorter and colder but I was happy to sometimes see a clear blue sky. Week after week, the city became completely white covered with snow and we could hear, during the nights and early mornings, the noise of the trucks removing the snow from the main streets of the city. It was also a warm feeling to be in my heated apartment and enjoy hot chocolate or warm soup while watching some people shoveling their driveways to be able to drive to their workplace. By the end of November, Vieux Québec was transformed into a real Christmas village. The streets were illuminated by the colorful Christmas lights and it was really enjoyable walking through the narrow streets covered in snow. I could not miss buying maple leaf syrup from the Christmas market, listening to local musicians in almost every corner of the old town and watching happy people skating around "Château Frontenac".

After the Christmas Holidays, I remember going one day to Laval University while a northern wind was blowing and the sky had a magic blue color. On my way to the bus stop, I met few people and they were completely wrapped up in warm clothes. That day the temperature reached -50^0C with the wind-chill factor and I felt my face burning. As I was walking very fast to avoid freezing, I thought that hell is not only about fire, but could actually be about extremely cold temperatures. I also learned during this long cold winter that patience is the best cure during hardship.

After the coldness of the winter comes the warmth and reward of spring. Indeed, at the end of the long winter, the melting snow, caused by warmer temperatures, in the different parts of the city announced spring as we could see the green grass again. Colorful flowers started to appear in different places of the city and some squirrels were playing in the parks around Laval University. It made me wonder what Paradise will be like! It was also strange to see people cycling and doing other sport activities at temperatures still around the freezing point.

"We will show them Our signs in the universe and in their own selves, until it becomes manifest to them that this (the Quran) is the truth." (Quran; 41:53)

Based on this Quranic verse, scientists around the planet have tried to find some universal laws such as statements that describe or predict a range of natural phenomena in the universe. In this matter, Allah (SWT) exhorts Muslims to observe and study the universe in order to find some signs of his Beautiful Names. For that reason, many verses of the Noble Quran invite Muslims to contemplate nature, and this has been interpreted to mean encouragement for scientific inquiry. According to Mr. Shamsher Ali, there are around 750 verses in the Noble Quran dealing with natural phenomena[5]. Moreover, I consider this Quranic verse "And of knowledge, you mankind have been given only a little." (Quran 17:85) as an inspiration for the acquisition of new knowledge. For some Muslim writers, the study of science stems from Al Tawheed[6]. This could be interpreted as only one divine science is governing the whole universe. In this perspective, my efforts (Ijtihad) in this book is to search for those Quranic verses that could lead me to the Divine

Science. In this perspective, listening to the lectures of Dr. Mohammed Rateb al-Nabulsi, led me to two Quranic verses.

The First Divine Law of Charity:
"And the heaven He has raised high, and has set up a Balance" (Quran; 55: 7)

Regarding this first Quranic verse, "The Fashioner" (SWT) created earth as a sphere and the sun heats equatorial regions more than polar regions. As a consequence, some regions in the planet are abundant in energy and other regions are deficient in energy. This uneven distribution of solar radiation is responsible for the imbalance of energy around the planet. According to this first Quranic verse, one can understand that Allah (SWT) has imposed some divine laws in order to set up a balance on earth. Because He is "The Giver of Justice" and "The All-Wise" (SWT), this equilibrium is established by driving matter and energy to move from places on earth, which have "concentrated" energy to regions on earth with "diluted" energy. This divine commandment is commonly known by physicists as the 2nd law of thermodynamics. Indeed, this law states that heat can be transferred only from higher temperatures to lower temperatures, fluids can flow only from higher pressures to lower pressures and rain falls from the sky to earth. Since this law is related to flows in nature, this aspect of the 2nd law of thermodynamics is defined in this book as the 1st universal law of dynamic systems and can simply be written as:

$$E_{High}\,(concentrated) \xrightarrow{\quad displacement \quad} E_{low}\,(diluted)$$

Equation (1)

"The seven heavens and the earth and all that is therein, glorify Him and there is not a thing but glorifies His Praise. But you understand not their glorification" (Quran; 17.44)

Moreover, based on this Quranic verse and considering energy as a richness, flows in the dynamic earth are therefore moving from regions rich (concentrated) in energy to regions poor (diluted) in energy. My spiritual vision of this physical phenomena tells me that "The Just One" (SWT) established a balance in the universe by imposing on places on earth rich in energy provided by Him using the sun, to share part of their richness with the regions of earth poor in energy. From this spiritual interpretation of movements in nature, the 1st universal law of dynamic systems is defined in this book as the 1st divine law of charity imposed by Allah (SWT) on the universe. Consequently, in concordance with the Quranic verse (55:7) under study, every single space rich in energy is glorifying Allah (SWT) by giving part of its richness (energy) to a poorer space in order to respect the balance imposed by Allah (SWT) on earth. As a result, equation (1) of dynamic systems becomes:

$$\textbf{Rich} \ (in \ energy) \xrightarrow{\textit{Divine Flow of Charity}} \textbf{Poor} (in \ energy)$$

Equation (2)

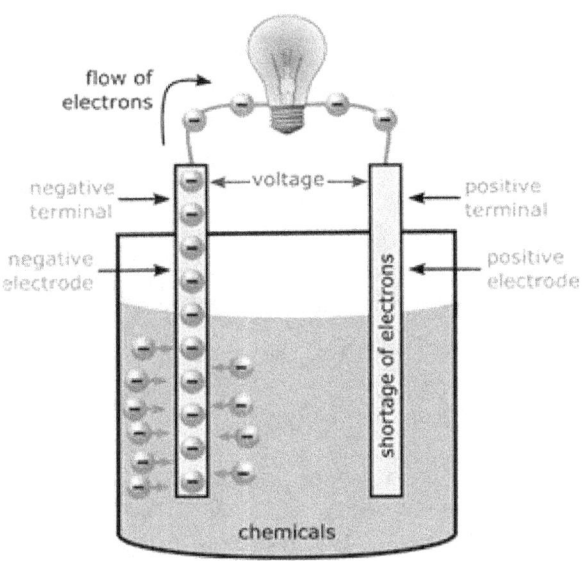

Figure 1: Electrical Battery

As shown in Figure 1, a typical example of the 1st divine law of charity is that the anode (rich in electrons) of an electrical battery is urged to give some electrons to the cathode (poor in electrons). In this case, the scientific explanation of the 1st divine law of charity is called the Electromotive force (Emf), which is defined as the characteristic of any "energy source" capable of moving electrons inside an electrical circuit.

The Second Divine Law of Charity:

"And there is not a thing but that with Us are its depositories, and We do not send it down except according to a known measure." (Quran; 15:21)

Secondly, from this Quranic verse, everything transported in the universe has a fixed measure determined by "The All Authoritative One" (SWT). Therefore, natural flows obey Allah (SWT) by always moving from places of "high energy" to places of "lower energy", and additionally their quantity and timing are also predestined by a second divine commandment. For example, according to the Quranic verse "And we sent down from the sky water in (due) measure." (Quran; 23:18), the amount of rain or snow (water) that falls, and its timing are predetermined by Allah (SWT). My efforts to find a scientific expression to this second Quranic verse (15:21) started in 1984, when I returned to Algeria from the USA in order to teach at the Algerian Petroleum Institute. During the industrial training of that academic year, the students were taken to a chemical plant located in the Western part of Algeria. To explain the common behavior of the different flows in the chemical plant to them, they were told that all dynamic systems follow the same scientific concept. They are generated by a "driving force" and are slowed down by a "resistance" caused by a solid or fluid located within the region.

In order to create a picture of this engineering concept in their mind, motivation was described to them as our "driving force" to go every day to the university to study to succeed in life. However, heavy rain could represent "resistance", causing us to drive slowly to college. Now, if the motivation to study is very strong, we may take the road even during very bad weather. On the other hand, if the class is boring, we will stay home even during a nice day. Following this analogy, it was explained to them that a flow is mathematically proportional to its driving force and inversely proportional to its resistance and the following qualitative general equation of dynamic systems was introduced:

$$Flow \propto \frac{Driving\ Force}{Resistance}$$

Equation (3)

In order to relate this general equation to the Quranic verse (15:21), the difference in energy between a region in earth having high energy (E_{High}) and a region having low energy (E_{low}) is considered as the "driving force" of any natural process and, the fluid or solid between these two regions presents a resistance "R" to the flow under consideration. Based on Equation (3), the flow of matter or energy transported could be qualitatively represented by:

$$Flow \left(\frac{Amount\ of\ matter\ or\ energy}{time} \right) \propto \frac{(E_{High} - E_{low})}{R}$$

Equation (4)

Equation (4) is defined in this book as the qualitative approach of the 2nd universal law of dynamic systems that deals with the amount of matter or energy to be transferred. In concordance with the 1st divine law of charity, Equation (4) is also the 2nd divine law of charity that determines the amount of transported matter or energy predetermined by Allah (SWT). Now, looking spiritually in the direction of the arrow in Figure 2, it could be perceived that heat (Q) is flowing from the hot part of the material "rich" in thermal energy $(T_2 > T_1)$ to the cold part of the metal "poor" in thermal energy.

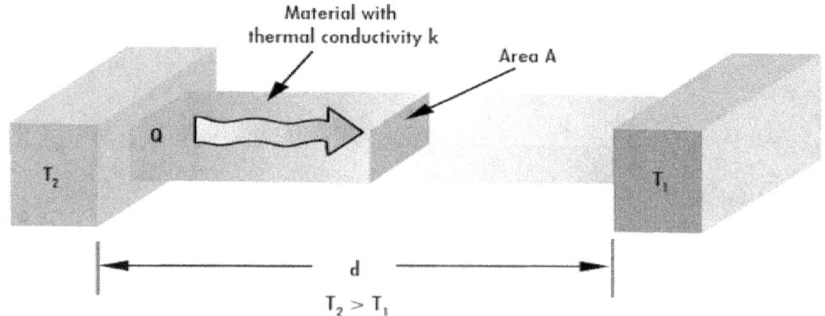

Figure 2: Heat transfer by conduction8.

Furthermore, as shown in Figure 2, the "gradient of richness" of heat (Q) is the difference in temperature $(T_2 - T_1)$ between the two parts of the material. If k is the thermal conductivity of the material, $(1/k)$ is therefore the resistance to the heat flow (Q). Based on the 2nd divine law of charity related to dynamic systems, the amount of richness (Q) given as charity can be qualitatively expressed by Equation (5):

$$Flow\ of\ richness \left(\frac{Q}{t}\right) \propto \frac{(T_2 - T_1)"Driving\ Force"}{\left(\frac{1}{k}\right)"Resistance"}$$

Equation (5)

Consequently, the second lesson to learn from meditating in nature is that Allah (SWT) imposes on every rich entity a requirement to share a prefixed amount of its richness with the poor in order to create justice and harmony between them. As described in Equation (6), Fourier's law is the quantitative expression of the amount of heat (Q) prefixed by the 2nd divine law of charity:

$$Heat\ flow \left(\frac{Q}{t}\right) = \frac{(T_2 - T_1)}{t/kA}$$

Equation (6)

24

Other examples of the scientific illustration of the 2nd divine law of charity are Fick's law in the Chemical Engineering field which measures the flow of matter conveyed by mass transfer by diffusion and Ohm's law in the electrical engineering field which is related to the flow of electrons.

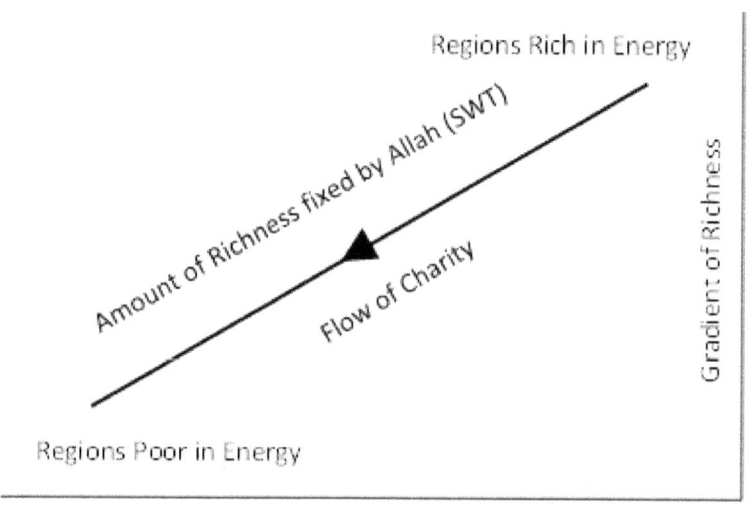

Figure 3: The Laws of the Divine Science

In conclusion, the 1st Quranic verse (55:7) taught me that in order to create a balance and harmony in nature, Allah (SWT) urges the regions rich in energy to give part of richness to the regions poor in energy. This is described in this book as 1st divine law of charity of the Divine Science. From the second Quranic verse (15:21), which is described as 2nd divine law of charity of the Divine Science, Allah

(SWT) also fixes the amount of the matter or energy to be flowing from a rich region to a poor region (Figure 3).

Signs of Charity and Spring in Nature

"Verily those who give alms, men or women, and lend Allah (SWT) a goodly loan, it shall be increased manifolds." (Quran; 57:18)

I spent my Christmas day of 1991 in Baie-Saint-Paul, a small town in the Quebec province of Canada. That morning, I went for a walk with my friend François through the narrow streets of the village adorned with art galleries and the few people we met on our way wished us "Joyeux Noël". When we reached the top of a hill, the brown and grey church located in the heart of the white village was very noticeable. I contemplated for some time the movements of the smoke leaving the chimneys of different homes as a heavy snow was falling slowly. Suddenly, I felt happy because I could imagine the quiet village as a pleased person offering a small gift from the warm heart (smoke from chimneys) to Allah (SWT) and receiving much more in return (heavy snow) from "The Most Appreciative" (SWT). On our way back to have lunch with my friend's parents, I remembered this Quranic verse "Who of you will lend Allah a goodly loan which He will return after multiplying it for him manifold. For Allah has the power both to decrease and increase, and to Him will you be returned" (Quran; 2:245).

"And We have made a shining lamp (sun). And We have sent down from the rainy clouds abundant water that We may produce therewith corn and vegetation and gardens of thick growth" (Quran; 78: 13-16)

Because of the existence of water, earth is unique among the other known celestial bodies. Indeed, water covers three-fourths of its surface and constitutes 60-70 % of the living world. At a micro level, the human body consists of more than 70% water[9]. The most amazing aspect about the divine science is that Allah (SWT) created water with some properties that allow it to regenerate and to be redistributed through evaporation and condensation in order to be endlessly renewable. The different stages of the water cycle (figure 4) are therefore described in this book because they are the demonstration that water is an infinitely renewable source of life. We can also perceive some Beautiful Names of Allah (SWT) and show how natural flows in the water cycle obey the divine laws of charity during the four seasons of the year.

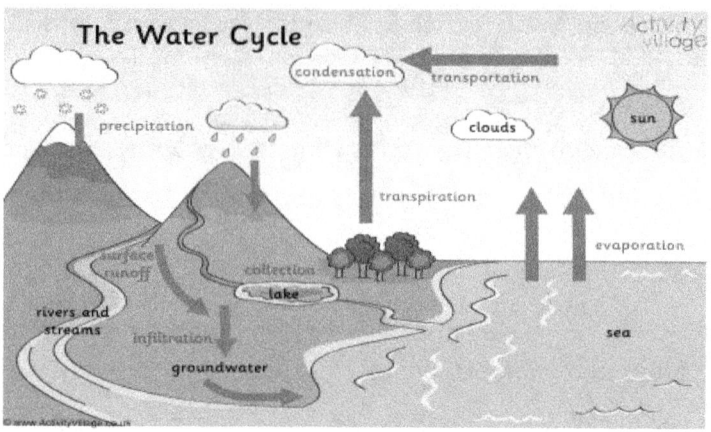

Figure 4: The Water Cycle10.

Evaporation of water using solar radiation

"And We have made (therein) a shining lamp (sun)"

(Quran; 78:13)

While people are enjoying sunshine during the summer season, the intense energy of the sun is also unnoticeably initiating the evaporation of water mainly from seas and oceans. This unseen natural process is the interpretation of the Beautiful Name "The Subtle One" of our Creator. For this first step of the water cycle, the 1st divine law of charity, introduced in the previous chapter, is fulfilled since the partial pressure of water vapor at the sea level has the highest value ($P_{w, sea}$) and decreases slowly to its lowest value ($P_{w, sky}$) located in the sky. Regarding the 2nd divine law of charity, the gradient of richness ($P_{w, sea} - P_{w, sky}$) between sea level and the sky is considered as the "driving force" of the evaporation process of water. Moreover, using the convective mass transfer coefficient (k_{air}) of atmospheric air, the flow of evaporation of water is regulated by the resistance to mass transfer ($1/k_{air}$) of the atmospheric air. Therefore, the flow of water evaporated is qualitatively expressed by the equation:

$$Flow\ of\ evaporation\ (WE) \propto \frac{(P_{w,sea} - P_{w,sky})}{\left(\dfrac{1}{k_{air}}\right)}$$

Equation (7)

In order to calculate the flow (WE), scientists in hydrometeorology use the Penman equation. The equation is based on measurements of the mean temperature of sea, wind speed, air pressure, and solar radiation.

Transportation of vapor using wind power

"And it is Allah Who sends the winds, so they can raise up the clouds, and We drive them to a dead land" (Quran; 35:9)

When the streets become lively again with happy children returning to classes, the winds of autumn start transporting clouds from over oceans to being over land. The power of the wind could be a small sign of the Beautiful Name "The Powerful" of our Creator. This second stage of the water cycle will obey the 1st divine law of charity when air over oceans will have higher values of atmospheric pressure (P_{High}) than the atmospheric pressure (P_{low}) of air over land. During this period of time and in order to utilize the 2nd divine law of charity, the gradient of richness (P_{High}- P_{low}) is taken as the driving force of the transportation process of clouds by the winds. The flow of transportation of water in the clouds is regulated by the friction (R_{air}) caused by atmospheric air. Therefore, similar to the evaporation process, the flow of transported of water by the winds (WT) could be qualitatively expressed by the equation:

$$Flow\ of\ transportation\ (WT) \propto \frac{(P_{High}-P_{low})}{R_{air}}$$

Equation (8)

The flow (WT) transported is usually quantified using the advection equation and the two most important parameters that affect the process are the strength and the angle of the wind.

Precipitation of rain and snow using earth's gravity

"He sends down water (rain) from the sky, and therewith revives the earth after its death" (Quran; 30:24)

When pedestrians start wrapping up in warm clothes, and the coldness of winter darkens the clouds, some places on earth experience rain and snow. As mentioned in the Quranic verse "And we made from water every living thing. Will they not then believe? (Quran; 21:30), Allah (SWT) made life possible on earth with water from the rain and snow. This is supposed to make us thankful to our Creator by remembering His Beautiful Name "The Provider". The last stage of the water cycle is bowing to the 1st divine law of charity because the water contained in heavy clouds has the highest value of potential energy (PE_{High}) and the value of their potential energy (PE_{low}) is lowest at the ground level. For the 2nd divine law of charity, the gradient of richness ($PE_{High} - PE_{low}$), caused by earth's gravity, is therefore the driving force of the precipitation process of water. It should be noted that the "The Bestower of Mercy" (SWT) created air with a resistance (R_{air}) that controls the speed of precipitation of the droplets of water. Without this resistance, rain could destroy vegetation and kill people as well as animals. Finally, the flow of precipitation of water (rain or snow) could be qualitatively described by the equation:

$$Flow\ of\ Precipitation\ (WF) \propto \frac{(PE_{High} - PE_{low})}{R_{air}}$$

Equation (9)

32

This amount (WF) is usually calculated by the "intensity of rainfall" which indicates the amount of rain that falls over time and it is measured in millimeters per hour (mm/h).

"Verily, in the heavens and the earth are signs for the believers" (Quran; 45: 3)

Based on this Quranic verse and contemplating the arrows in Figure 4 from a spiritual perspective, it could be concluded that the direction of the flows in the water cycle is from a region rich in energy to a region poor in energy. This is a clear sign of obedience of nature to the 1st divine law of charity as indicated in the first Quranic verse (55:7). For the 2nd divine law of charity, as mentioned in the Quranic verse (15:21) of the previous chapter, the divine purpose of the seas and oceans is to use solar energy in order to generate a certain flow of water vapor (WE), predetermined by Allah (SWT), as charity to the dry skies over the seas and oceans. Following this step, the sky over the oceans becomes rich enough in water. It has then its divine duty to utilize the power of wind in order to offer a certain part of that flow of water (in the clouds), predesignated by Allah (SWT), as charity to the dry skies over the lands. Finally, when the sky over the land also gets rich enough in water (heavy clouds), its divine purpose is to use the earth's gravity in order to offer a portion of water as rain or snow (WF), predestined by Allah

(SWT), as charity to the dry land. In conclusion, since nature was created to be a universal school for humanity and as mentioned in the Quranic verses (55:7 and 15:21), all the natural flows are fulfilling the two divine laws of charity imposed by Allah (SWT).

> "See you not that Allah sends down rain (rain) from the sky, and causes it to penetrate the earth, as water springs, and afterward thereby produces crops of different colours; and afterward they wither and you see them turn yellow then He makes them dry and broken piece" (Quran; 39: 21)

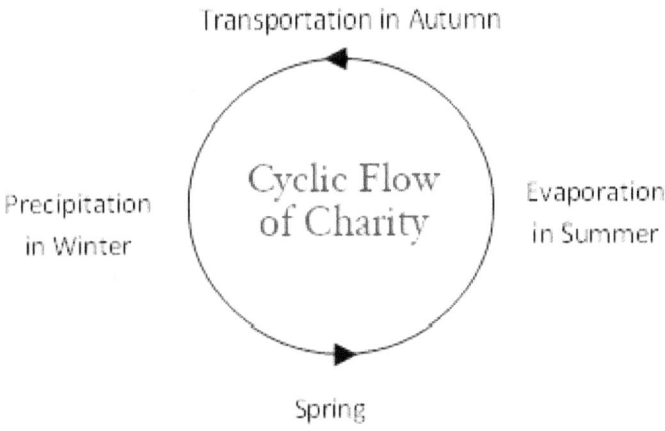

Figure 5: Cyclic Flow of Charity and Spring

Indeed, after the hot summer, the windy autumn and the cold winter, nature seems happy again during the lovely spring. By His Beautiful Names "The Most Generous" and "The Sustainer", it is a time of abundance and regeneration, with birds singing and flowers blooming. Just as Allah (SWT) brings the dead to life, the earth infuses the flowers and blossoms with new life. At the end of this paradisiac spring, nature seems to lose balance as the cycle of charities start again (Figure 5).

My spiritual thought teaches me that spring is a reward from Allah (SWT) to every single creature in nature after the Cyclic Flow of Charity.

The Soul of Islam and the
Eternal Path of Charity

"When the Event befalls. And there can be no denial of its befalling. Bringing low and exalting. When the earth will be shaken with a terrible shake. And the mountains will be powdered to dust." (Quran; 56:1-6)

During the first hours of January 17th of 1995, I was suddenly awakened by a strong noise and the walls of my room were shaking for some time. When the trembling stopped, I quickly left the apartment and saw all my neighbors in the street. I learned that a major earthquake had hit the city of Kobe. When I went to work that morning, the streets were empty and the research center was closed. During the weeks following the quake, some colleagues were absent because some roads and highways around Kobe were damaged. During this period, my Japanese neighbor advised me to buy a lot of food because many people from Kobe were shopping in our town. About two months later, I saw several buses taking workers from Ikeda to help clear the debris of the collapsed and badly damaged buildings and homes in Kobe.

During the period of spring of 1995, my Japanese friend Haruto invited me to visit Kobe to see the damage done by the earthquake. Early morning, we took the train from Osaka station. Because the railroad tracks were buckled and twisted around Kobe, the train stopped in a small village located a few miles from Kobe. From there, we continued our trip by bus to the suburbs of the city. The scenes of damage were everywhere as Kobe seemed like a bombarded city in a war movie. Many neighborhoods were totally destroyed and I noticed that the typical Japanese homes with a heavy roof had not survived the earthquake. The major freeway of the city had collapsed, and many buildings had been uplifted. I saw people selling food and water in the streets and some visitors secretly taking pictures of the devastation. When I arrived at the city's mosque, I realized that the mosque and nearby church were not affected by the earthquake. After praying, we went back to take the bus and return to Ikeda. On our way, I stopped in front of the ruins of a home because I noticed a small book under the debris. When I opened it, there were many smiles and colorful pictures. Suddenly my eyes filled with tears realizing that the child who had been reading this book died in a sudden and terrible way. This sad feeling did not leave me for some weeks and I shared the unhappy event with my colleagues at my workplace. Listening to the news on the television, I learned that more 6500 people died in the earthquake. Indeed, as

Allah (SWT) is "The Giver of Life", He is also "The Bringer of Death" as mentioned in the Quranic verse "O you who have believed, fear Allah as He should be feared and do not die except as Muslims [in submission to Him]" (Quran; 3:102). Therefore, since this inescapable death can knock at our door at any moment of our life, the most important question is "How to prepare ourselves for the everlasting life in Paradise?"

"Verily man was created very impatient. Irritable when evil touches him and niggardly when good touches him. Expect those who are devoted to prayers. And those in whose wealth there is a recognized right for the beggars who ask and for the unlucky who have lost their property and wealth…" (Quran; 70: 19-25)

In contradiction to the fact that the nature was created to obey the divine laws of charity imposed by Allah (SWT) and the reward is the lovely season of spring, human beings are born with the ability to think and free to fulfill or not the divine duty of charity during their social or professional activities. My understanding is that the first part of this Quranic verse is related to people who follow their natural instinct and try to accomplish activities that benefit only them. In contrary, the second part concerns those who fight this selfish tendency with patience because they understand that they are born with the divine obligation to worship "The Creator" (SWT) by practicing the five pillars of Islam and accomplish the duties of charity by helping others.

> "You are the best community (Ummah) raised up for (the benefit of) humanity; enjoining what is right and forbidding what is wrong and believing in God." (Quran; 3:110)

As a Muslim, I belong to my Ummah (Muslim community). Muslims around the world are like one family from different backgrounds and ethnic groups. The purpose of the life of Muslims is to serve Allah (SWT) alone as the One God. The religion of Islam is a complete code of life that firmly supports the concept of human well-being and urges every Muslim to behave in a consequential manner. The noblest message of morality is to respect the civil liberties of every individual in society while defining the duties of each person to perform in every aspect of life in order to create and nurture a peaceful and serene environment. Because of that, Allah (SWT) refers to the Ummah as the best community and enjoining what is right (Allah (SWT) calls it al-ma'roof because the sound Fitrah knows it) and forbidding what is wrong (al-munkar) is one of the noblest Islamic answerabilities. One of the biggest causes of the destruction of nations before Islam is that they did not forbid evil (al-munkar) or enjoin the good (al ma'roof). Consequently, when Muslims turn away from their faith and not forbidding evil or enjoining the good, they lose their quality of being best community. They are therefore a nation like any other nation that Allah (SWT) created. Therefore, if the Ummah fails to adopt this responsibility, wrongdoing and corruption will spread and we will deserve punition from Allah (SWT).

In order to prevent us from doing things He has forbidden, such as shedding blood, committing adultery, drinking alcohol, oppressing people and consuming our wealth unlawfully, Allah (SWT) blessed us with Al-Eaql as guidance in order to find His signs around us and Al-Fitrah to overcome selfishness and help others. Moreover, He also describes Himself in the Noble Quran and the sayings of the Prophet (PBUH) with Ninety-Nine Beautiful Name in order to adopt Al-Tawheed.

"He grants wisdom to whom He wills; and he to whom wisdom is granted is indeed granted abundant good. But none remember except men of understanding" (Quran; 2:269)

Al Eaql: Could be considered as the unseen authority of thinking and logic. The Noble Quran has put a great amount of importance on using Al Eaql to reach wisdom in all aspects of our life including gaining awareness about the existence of Allah (SWT), knowing good from evil, differentiating between truth and lies, knowing the difference between freedom and domination, following the moral and leaving the immoral and finally to find purpose in life. Wisdom is a positive term used repeatedly in the Noble Quran as a characteristic of the righteous. By His Beautiful Name "The Wise One", Allah (SWT) gives wisdom to people as cited in this Quranic verse. And as the Prophet (PBUH) said: "The word of wisdom is the lost property of the believer. Wherever he finds it, he is most deserving of it."[11], we can obtain wisdom if we value knowledge, are open to learning by listening to Islamic lessons, and we welcome correction and discipline. Looking at my travel experiences, we can also gain wisdom by learning from other cultures and religions that can help us understand Islam from different angles. Another way to achieve a state of wisdom is to contemplate nature and all Allah (SWT)'s creatures and learn with a thoughtful heart.

"So, direct your face toward the religion, inclining to truth. Adhere to the Al-Fitrah of Allah upon which He has created all people" (Quran; 30:30)

Al-Fitrah: Human beings are born with an innate inclination of Al Tawheed, which is encapsulated in the sound Fitrah along with compassion, intelligence, kindness and all other attributes that embody the concept of humanity. Because of their Fitrah, human beings deny evil (al munkar) without education, without guidance, without studying, and accept what is good (al ma'roof). With reference to this concept, new research findings in the field of human biology show that we may be born to be sociable and have the urge to help[12]. Therefore, Al Fitrah could be interpreted as the Quran-coded DNA that every human is imprinted with from birth. Al-Fitrah could also be considered as the inner voice of an Angel that guides every new-born and child in order to be happy in life by fulfilling the divine duties they are born for and live eternally in Paradise after the soul leaves the body. Unfortunately, when we grow up, a second voice emerges to compete with the first naïve one and adults become more selective in helping others and tend to become more selfish. They are more attracted by material comfort to enjoy life, competition between people becomes more prevalent, and crimes and wars are globally evident. Regarding this second voice, the Noble Quran says "And Satan will say when the matter has been decided: Verily Allah promised you a promise of truth. And I too promised you, but I betrayed you. I had no authority over you except that I called you and you responded to me" (Quran; 14:22). Based on this verse, following the hidden voice of Satan is the reason we sometimes ignore following our divine duties. In order to guide us with a warning, Allah (SWT) says "Allah burdens not a person beyond his scope. He gets reward for the good which he has earned, and he is punished for that evil which he has earned (Quran 2: 286).

"Allah does not forgive that anything should be associated with Him, but He forgives anything other than this to whomsoever He pleases; and whoever associates anything with Allah, he devises indeed a great sin." (Quran; 4:48)

Al-Tawheed: Means the non-existence of coincidence and that the pathways of our lives do not happen by chance. It is assurance that our entire lives depend on our relationship with Allah (SWT) alone. Al Eaql and Al-Fitrah are fundamental paths to realize the reality of Al-Tawheed. Moreover, as mentioned in this Quranic verse "God was gracious to the believers when he raised up among them a messenger from themselves who recite to them the verses of his book (Noble Quran) and shows them his signs, purifies them, and instructs them in the book of wisdom. They were evidently in manifest misguidance." (Quran; 3:164), Allah (SWT) also sent Prophet Muhammad (PBUH), as He sent all previous Prophets to guide humanity to Him.

Allah (SWT) is the Almighty, Creator and Sustainer of the universe, Who is similar to nothing and nothing is comparable to Him. When The Prophet (PBUH) was asked by his companions about Allah (SWT); the answer came directly from Him in the form of a short chapter of the Noble Quran, which is considered the essence of the unity or the motto of Al Tawheed. This is chapter 112 which reads: "Say (O Muhammad) He is God the One God, the Everlasting Refuge, who has not begotten, nor has been begotten, and equal to Him is not anyone." (Quran; 112). In order to help us adopt Al-Tawheed and obey Him during all our social and professional activities, Allah (SWT) has revealed His Ninety-Nine Beautiful Names repeatedly in the Noble Quran and in the sayings of prophet Muhammad (PBUH). Moreover, Allah (SWT) created us with five senses in order to experience the world around us and find His signs. Indeed, the universe is like a silent Quran with so many marks of the Beautiful Names of Allah (SWT). For example, knowing that there are stars billions of light years from earth is certainly a sign to glorify Him by His Beautiful Name "The Magnificent". Watching the beautiful smile of a mother holding her baby is a sign of the Love of Allah (SWT) for all human beings by His Beautiful Name "The Most Loving". Listening to the waves crashing against the cliffs will remind us of His Beautiful Name "The All-Strong". The beauty of nature during spring could be a sign of the magnificence of Heaven and His Beautiful Name "Lord of Majesty and Generosity". Finally, the chilly winter or hot summer could be signs to fear the punishment of hell and His Beautiful Name "The Reckoner". Muslims should therefore make efforts to know the meaning of The Beautiful Names of Allah (SWT) and live by them in order to always feel His presence.

" (O Muhammad), put your trust in Him Who is Ever-Living, Who will never die, and glorify Him with His praise. He suffices as the Knower of the sins of His servants," (Quran; 25:58)

Those who understand and live with the idea of Al Tawheed, have strong faith that Allah (SWT) alone controls everything in the universe and every human being on earth behind the visible material world. Therefore, they depend only upon Allah (SWT) and trust Him (Al-Tawakkul). However, Al-Tawakkul means that we should always obey all the divine laws imposed by Allah (SWT) on the universe. In this topic, Anas ibn Malik reported: A man said, "O Messenger of Allah, should I tie my camel and trust in Allah, or should I leave her untied and trust in Allah?" The Prophet, peace and blessings be upon him, said, "Tie her and trust in Allah"[13]. For example, if we are sick, we need first to visit the best doctor possible and, trusting that Allah (SWT) is the only healer, we can give charity and ask Allah (SWT) in invocation to give the doctor the necessary knowledge and wisdom to find the best treatment for us.

"Verily Allah enjoins justice and to be patient in performing your duties to Allah" (Quran; 16:90)

In concordance with the two Quranic verses (55:7 and 15:21) of the previous chapter related to the divine science in nature, in this

Quranic verse related to humanity, Allah (SWT) also orders justice between people and urges them to perform their divine duties with patience. In this perspective, it is very important to note that the Arabic word Sadaqah (charity) originates from the word "tasdik" which means approval of our Muslim faith. Therefore, as mentioned in this Quranic verse "Whatever wealth you spend in charity is to your own benefit for you spend merely to please Allah "(Quran; 2:272), I have come to understand that the 1st divine law of charity for Muslims corresponds to our intention to please only Allah (SWT) during our interactions with people, animals and plants. For the same purpose of the Quranic verse (Quran; 55:7) to the universe, the goal of the 1st divine law of charity for humanity, mentioned in the Quranic verse (16:90), is to establish an atmosphere of justice between the rich and the poor and harmony in our societies. Moreover, similar to the 2nd divine law of charity for the universe (Quran; 15:21), the second part of the Quranic verse (16:90) is related to our divine duties to help others by fighting our selfishness. On the other hand, if the Cyclic Flow of Charity in nature ends every year with spring, all our actions in helping people, animals and plants during our social or professional activities will be added as good deeds to our eternal soul in the Eternal Path of Charity.

For instance, prayer is the second pillar of Islamic practice and worship. The Arabic word Salat (prayer) derives from the word šilat (connection) which means it creates a spiritual link between the servants and Allah (SWT). My understanding is that the 1st divine law in prayers to please Allah (SWT) is humility, devotion and concentration (Al-Khushū) during prayer. This state of mind helps us to connect with Allah (SWT)'s Mercy and benefit from His Generosity. For the 2nd divine law of charity for Muslims, the five daily obligatory prayers will be added as good deeds in the Eternal Path of Charity. Moreover, in this Quranic verse "(O Prophet)!" Take alms out of their riches and thereby cleanse them and bring about their growth (in righteousness), and pray for them. Indeed, your prayer is a source of tranquility for them. Allah is All-Hearing, All-Knowing" (Quran; 9:103), Allah (SWT) also asks us to show our intention to please Him by sharing part of the wealth He provided to us with the less fortunate in order to purify our soul in the Eternal Path of charity. Indeed, the Arabic word Zakat means to self-purify our soul. From this definition, the 1st divine law of charity of wealth (Zakat Al mal) is the intention of every rich person to please Allah (SWT) and self-purify his/her soul in the Eternal Path of Charity by helping the poor. For the 2nd divine law of charity, the amount of charity is fixed at 2.5% of a Muslim's total savings and wealth above a minimum amount (nisab) is donated annually[14].

In addition to this obligation, we can have the opportunity to self-purify our soul and add good deeds in the Eternal Path of Charity by giving as charity whatever we can as cited in the Noble Quran "They ask you (O Muhammad) what they should spend. Say: Whatever you spend of good must be for parents and kindred and orphans and the needy and for wayfarers, and whatever you do of good deeds, Allah knows it well" (Quran; 2:215). This Quranic verse means that the intention to please Allah (SWT) and self-purify our soul in the Eternal Path of Charity is not limited to only helping those in need by giving them money or food to survive, but encompasses acts of charity such as offering assistance and time to relatives, neighbors and friends as well as those who are unwell to comfort them and perhaps add some joy to their life, or enhance it in some way. For example, being kind and considerate towards relatives, neighbors and coworkers are also good deeds as mentioned in the Quranic verse "Worship God and join none with Him in worship, and do good to parents, kinsfolk, orphans, the needy, the neighbor who is near of kin, the neighbor who is a stranger, the companion by your side, the wayfarer (you meet) and those whom your right hands possess. Verily, Allah does not like such as are proud and boastful." (Quran; 4:36).

Moreover, Prophet Mohamed (PBUH) teaches us that the Eternal Path of Charity has many doors as he said: "Charity is prescribed for each descendant of Adam every day the sun rises." He was then asked: "From what do we give charity every day?" The Prophet replied: "The doors of goodness are many: enjoining good, forbidding evil, removing harm from the road, listening to the deaf, leading the blind, guiding one to the object of his need, hurrying with the strength of one's legs to one in sorrow who is asking for help, and supporting the feeble with the strength of one's arms. All of these are charity prescribed for you. He then said: "Even your smile for your brother is a charity"[15].

On a last note, as mentioned in this Quranic verse "And We have sent you forth [O Muhammad] not but as a mercy for mankind and jinn" (Quran; 21:107), Prophet Muhammad (PBUH) was sent as a divine gift of mercy for the whole of mankind until the Day of Judgment. For this mission of love and compassion, The Prophet Muhammad (PBUH) emphasized love, sympathy and kindness towards all mankind as he said "Verily, Allah is gentle and He loves gentleness. He rewards for gentleness what is not granted for harshness and He does not reward anything else like it."[16]. In another beautiful saying, the Prophet (PBUH) has said: "None among you is a true believer unless he loves for others what he loves for himself."[17].

"There is no creature on the earth or bird that flies with its wings but that they are communities like you (Quran; 6:38)

Moreover, based on this Quranic verse, treating animals with kindness and mercy is just one of the responsibilities of every Muslim. To illustrate this further, The Prophet (PBUH) told this story: "A man felt very thirsty while he was on the way, there he came across a well. He went down the well, quenched his thirst and came out. Meanwhile he saw a dog panting and licking mud because of excessive thirst. He said to himself, 'This dog is suffering from thirst as I did.' So, he went down the well again and filled his shoe with water and watered the dog. Allah thanked him for that deed and forgave him. His followers said: "O Allah's Messenger! Is there a reward for us in serving the animals?" He replied: "Yes, there is a reward for serving any animate (living being)."[18].

"Now, behold! Your Lord said to the angels: I am placing upon the earth a human successor to steward it" (Quran; 2:30)

This Quranic verse teaches us that mankind's relationship and responsibility to the earth is also seen as that of a custodian. For example, as cited in this Quranic verse: "Eat and drink of that which Allah has provided and do not act corruptly, making mischief on the earth" (Quran 2: 60), a Muslim must not be extravagant in consumption, whether of food, cloth or natural resources. Moreover, Prophet Muhammad (PBUH) also encourages the growing of plants by saying: "If a Muslim plants a tree or grow grains and a bird, a person or an animal eats from it will be counted as a charity for him."[19].

The Eternal Path of Charity in Workplaces

"Your Lord has decreed that you worship none but Him, and that you be kind to parents. Whether one or both of them attain old age in your life, say not to them a word of contempt, nor repel them, but address them in terms of honor. "And, out of kindness, lower to them the wing of humility, and say: 'My Lord! Bestow on them your Mercy even as they cherished me in childhood" (Quran; 17:23-24)

After my graduate studies at Stevens Institute of Technology in Hoboken (NJ, USA), I went back to Algeria in January 1984 to teach at the Algerian Petroleum Institute. During my first academic year as a teacher, I shared an apartment with another colleague. After my military service, the school decided to distribute some apartments to teachers to encourage them to stay in the institute. When, I entered my apartment, I found it small and I was worried that it would be too narrow if I had children. During that summer of 1987, I went to visit my grandmother in my hometown Beni-Saf, a port city located in the western part of Algeria. As usual, she was very happy to welcome me into her small room and we had fun talking about the stories and the funny things that had happened to me in New York City. I also told her that the first thing I felt sad about is not hearing the call for prayers even before feeling the absence of my parents and brothers and sisters. At that moment, we heard the call from the mosque and she went into the corner of the room to pray. After she finished her prayer, our discussion became more serious and she told me that it was time for me to find a nice lady and have a family. When I took this opportunity to complain about my narrow apartment, she seemed worried but reminded me this Quranic verse: "Verily, Allah is with the patient" (Quran; 2:153). I smiled as I understood that I needed to learn how to create space in my heart, so I can find it even in my small apartment. At the end of my visit, when I kissed her to say goodbye, she took my hand and recited this meaningful Quranic verse "If you give thanks, I will certainly grant you more" (Quran; 14:7). Since she died, I am praying to "The Merciful" (SWT) to give her a large space in Paradise.

> "Allah has favoured some of you with more worldly provisions than others. Then those who are more favoured do not give away their provisions to their slaves lest they become equal sharers in it. Do they, then, deny the favour of Allah?" (Quran; 16:71)

My understanding is that, aligned with the way Allah (SWT) conceived the universe with different "gradients of richness" including energy, pressure, temperature, altitude and concentrations of different substances, He also created us within a "gradient of wealth" like finances, material elements, health, appearance, intelligence to learn and the ability to master different skills. The "Wise One" (SWT) knows that this innate "gradient" of abilities and skills between people is needed to create different types of jobs and professions so people can help each other. For example, in hospitals, surgeons, doctors and nurses are all needed with their different skills and abilities in the treatment of sick people, and together they create a comprehensive or full treatment plan for the patient. They are all integral to the whole, and could be visualized as each being a spoke in a wheel, with all parts being required to form the whole. Similarly, in research centers, researchers, experts, engineers and technicians are all vital, based on their abilities. Professors and lecturers are essential in universities and teachers are needed in primary and secondary schools. Finally, laborers are also required in industry to carry out physical labor in order to build infrastructures.

"And He has raised in ranks, some above others the He may try you in that which He has bestowed you" (Quran; 6:165)

Moreover, based on this Quranic verse, in order to obey the 1st divine law of charity, Muslims are urged to use their inborn abilities with the only intention to please Allah (SWT) by helping others and self-purify their soul in the Eternal Path of Charity. As a consequence, their daily duties will be counted as good deeds.

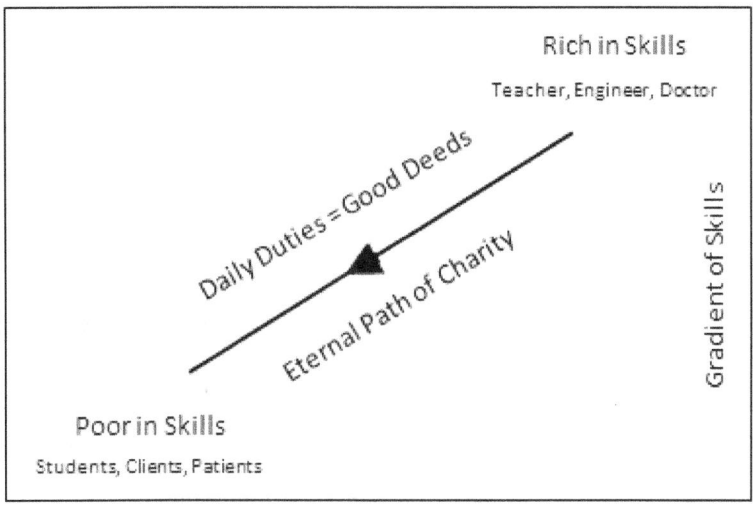

Figure 6: Eternal Path of Charity in Workplaces

For example, as shown in Figure 6, the divine duty of an engineer is to offer expertise as charity to properly solve technical problems. The divine purpose of a doctor is to treat patients adequately and provide them with the proper diagnosis and treatment and the divine responsibility of a teacher is to impart knowledge and enable students to learn. In general, by fulfilling the 1st divine law of charity to please Allah (SWT), all our daily professional and social activities while interacting with people, animals and plants will be counted as good deeds in the Eternal Path of Charity.

On a larger scale, organizations are social units of people, including a management structure that determines relationships between different activities and members, which subdivides and assigns roles, responsibilities, and the authority to carry out different tasks[20]. In any organization, each level of the hierarchy requires specific hard skills and soft skills to adequately fulfil the role, and people are generally selected based on these two characteristics: Hard skills are mainly the three elements of the KSA (Knowledge, Skills and Abilities). On the other hand, the soft skills are related to Communication, Teamwork, Adaptability, Problem-Solving, Creativity, Work Ethic, Interpersonal Skills and Time Management. The importance of soft skills is demonstrated by the fact that that the quality of interactions between employees affect the efficiency of the workflow at all levels of the organization.

In order to maximize the quality of interaction between company personnel and the efficiency of the workflow, the objective of workforce management (WFM) is to facilitate the ranking of all members of the hierarchy to match their skills in order to reduce internal tensions and the full potential of employees is realized. On the other hand, if employees are incorrectly ranked, they could be a source of friction in the hierarchy. Traci Moxson elaborates that "it's clear that the time has come for organizations to put substance behind the phrase 'people are our most important asset' and genuinely deliver right skills, right place, right time!" [21].

"Indeed, in the Messenger of Allah (Muhammad) you have a good example to follow for him who hopes for Allah and the Last Day and remembers Allah much." (Quran; 33: 21)

Regarding the Islamic approach to management of organizations, the first mission of the Prophet (PBUH) was to build a mosque in Medina that served as the first community house for Muslims. It served as the command center of leadership and a social center. His next duty was to establish a bond of brotherhood and mutual aid between the believers by saying "The parable of the believers in their affection, mercy, and compassion for each other is that of a body. When any limb aches, the whole body reacts with sleeplessness and fever."[22]. Therefore, in order to solve the economic problems of Medina, he proposed the believers from Medina (Ansar) should share their trade and wealth with the believers (Muhajereen) who left their wealth in Mecca. Prophet Muhammad (PBUH) also established in Medina a strong state on the basis of peace, solidarity, and harmony between the Muslims, Jews, Christians, disbelievers, as well as a group of hypocrites. The covenant required that all citizens are duty-bound to protect the city, share the common obligation of caring for and aiding one another, and enjoin what is good for the nation and ward off whatever may threaten it[23].

Mecca was not only the center of pilgrimage during the pre-Islamic and post-revelation era, but it was also known as center of commerce and economic activities. Additionally, there were many successful businessmen amongst the Companions of the Prophet (PBUH) such as 'Uthman, Abdurrahman Ibn 'Awf and Zubayr Ibn al-'Awwam and others. The study of their approaches in businesses shall enlighten us with the recipes of success in business development based on the two basic principle of al-adl (justice) and al-ihsan (charity/improvement)[24]. Finally, the Noble Quran has stressed the importance of fairness in business as Allah (SWT) says "And, O my people, give full measure and weight justly, and defraud not men of their things, and act not corruptly in the land making mischief. What remains with Allah is better for you, if you are believers" (Quran; 11: 85-86).

"If there were in the heavens and the earth, other gods, besides Allah, there would have been collision in both." *(Quran; 21:22)*

First, this Quranic verse demonstrates the significance and requirement of unity of command and unity of direction. Therefore, following the Islamic tradition, this book proposes the application of the two divine laws of charity in order to optimize the workforce management in Muslim organizations. In the beginning, identical to the patterns of "natural flows" in the water cycle, there are also "workflows" and "interactions" between employees at all levels of the hierarchy. Therefore, in order to be able to apply the divine science, similar to the "gradient of energy" in nature, there is a need to have a "gradient of skills" in the hierarchy. For this purpose, the selected managers at the top of the administration should have the highest of abilities and expertise in all the needed skills and employees at the bottom of the hierarchy should have the lowest abilities and skills to perform the duties.

"We raise some of them above others in ranks, so that some may command work from others" (Quran; 43:32)

Secondly, this Quranic verse contains the whole attitude and insight of modern management. It highlights, in essence, the creation of appropriate hierarchies and the division of responsibilities subject to individual capabilities. Therefore, in order to create equity between employees, personnel with intermediate skills should be in the appropriate rank of the hierarchy in order to be able to help by giving proper advice and instruction, as well as guidance to employees under their supervision. In this topic, literature has shown that helping others to become successful will remove the obstacles, excessive bureaucracy, interpersonal conflict, uncertainty and toxic cultures that hinder success[25]. Moreover, a study found that when people engaged in reactive helping (helping when asked), they received more gratitude. In turn, the helpers perceived that they had a greater impact and felt more engaged at work the next day[26].

It should be noted that, in this Islamic model of workforce management, it is considered that all soft skills of employees are linked to the 1st divine law of charity. Which means that the intention to please Allah (SWT) is the only reason for helping employees under supervision. According to the literature, properly helping employees under supervision could be the result of the following advice:

> Present a smiling face to them because Prophet Muhammad (PBUH) was always cheerful and bright-faced. According to historians he always kept smiling in the face of his Companions to the extent that Abdullah ibn Al-Harith ibn Hazm said, "I have never seen anyone who smiles more than the Prophet does."[27].

Show also kindness to them during professional interactions and discussions as Prophet Muhammad (PBUH) said, "The best among you are those who have the best manners and character"[28].

Be thankful to Allah (SWT) during good interactions with people and be patient during times of hardship and pain as Prophet Mohamed (PBUH) said "Wondrous is the affair of the believer for there is good for him in every matter and this is not the case with anyone except the believer. If he is happy, then he thanks Allah and thus there is good for him, and if he is harmed, then he shows patience and thus there is good for him."[29].

O you who believe! Do your duty to Allah and fear Him. And seek the means of approach to Him, and strive hard in His cause so you might be successful." (Quran; 5:35)

First, let us assume the difference of position between a manager (Position High) and subordinates (Position low) in the hierarchy of any organization to be positive. Now, if the manager has higher expertise (Rich in skills) than the employees (Poor in skills) under his/her supervision, it will result positive values of the efficiency of the workflow at this level of the organization:

$$Efficiency\ of\ workflow \propto \frac{(Rich_{skills} - Poor_{skills})}{Position_{High} - Position_{low}} > 0$$

Equation (10)

Moreover, if the manager is willing to fulfill the 1st divine law of charity by helping team members, the manager can self-purify his/her soul in the Eternal Path of Charity. For the 2nd divine law of charity, the workflow performed by the help of this manager will be counted for him/her as charity (Figure 7).

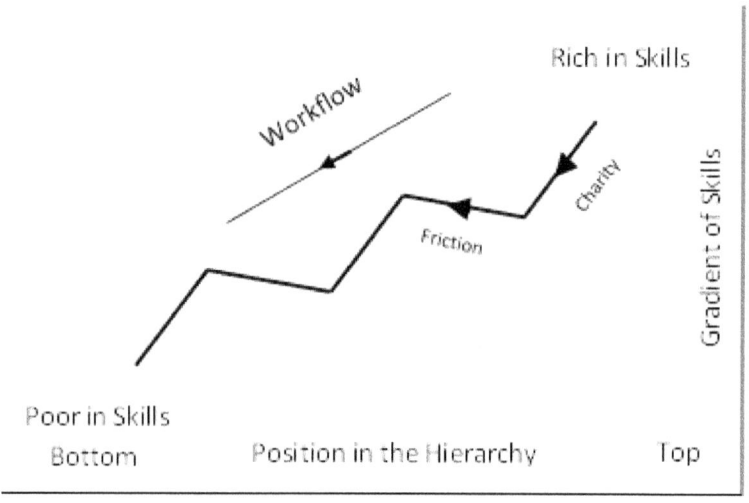

Figure 7: Some Employees in Wrong Position

However, if some employees in positions of authority and more responsibility have to provide leadership to coworkers who are in a lower position (Position low) but equipped with higher hard skills

(Rich in skills), it will result negative values of the efficiency of the workflow due to friction during their interactions (Figure 7).

$$Efficiency\ of\ workflow\ \propto \frac{Poor_{skills} - Richll_{skills}}{Position_{High} - Position_{low}} < 0$$

Equation (11)

Because these managers cannot help the other team members, they will not be able to please Allah (SWT) and fulfill their 1st divine duty of charity. On the contrary, these managers could feel frustrated and use fear and humiliation to show their authority. This nonprofessional behavior will cause the low morale of subordinates and reduce their level of engagement. In other words, the negative values of the equation (11), caused by employees incorrectly placed within the ranking system, are similar to adding extra resistance to the workflow. This will have the potential to affect the efficiency of workflow in the hierarchy and the overall performance of the company in a negative way. Therefore, based on this proposed Islam-based model and similar to the direction of natural flows, if every employee is in the right position according the hard skills (Figure 8) and is willing to please Allah (SWT) and fulfill the 1st divine law of charity by helping teammates under supervision, it will result in minimum frictions between employees and boost the morale and engagement of all personnel.

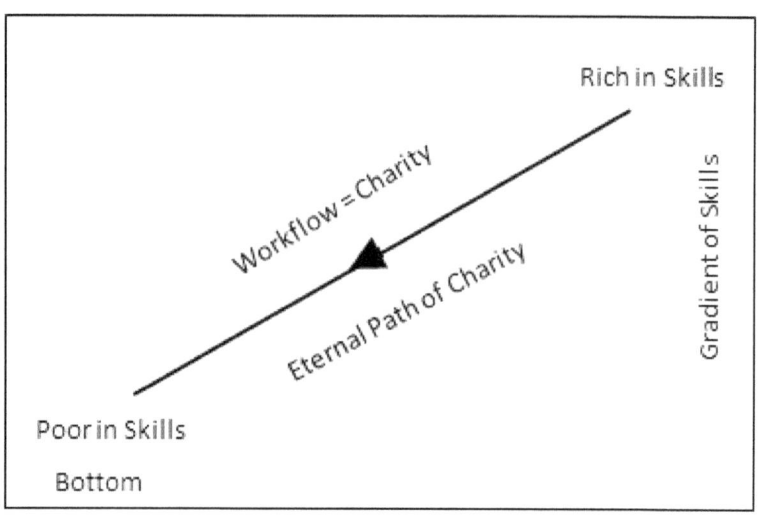

Figure 8: Eternal Path of Charity in Organizations

As a result, the efficiency of the workflow at each level of the organization will have maximum positive values. Moreover, the employees who were helped are more likely to help others in return. As a result, workplaces with helping cultures see better employee performance. Research also suggests that more helpful workplaces actually perform better; they produce better-quality products and have increased sales[26]. Therefore, by integrating the divine laws of charity in any organization, it will result in the highest performance of the company due to the smoothest workflows. Finally, as Allah says: "As for him who gave out his wealth (for Allah's sake) and abstained (from disobeying Him), and affirmed the Truth of goodness, We shall facilitate for him the Way to Bliss" (Quran; 92-5:7), similar to the beautiful spring after the gestures of charity in nature, the reward for the managers who please Allah (SWT) and fulfill the 1st divine law of charity is certainly happiness. This divine recompense will allow them create an enjoyable environment in the workplace. For the 2nd divine law of charity, the workflow performed by the help of these managers will be counted as their good deeds in the Eternal Path of Charity.

> On a last note, with His Infinite Mercy, Allah (SWT) required Muslims to worship Him in workplaces by helping others only to count our daily duties as good deeds in the Eternal Path of Charity. At the same time, He also reassures us that He is our only provider for all our wealth, including salary as mentioned in the Noble Quran "And no moving creature is there on earth but its provision is due from Allah. And He knows its dwelling place and its deposit. All is in a Clear Book." (Quran; 11:6).

Islam-based Leadership in Workplaces

"Say: 'O Allah, Lord of all dominion! You give dominion to whom You will, and take away dominion from whom You will, and You exalt whom You will, and abase whom You will. In Your Hand is all good. Surely You are All-Powerful."
(Quran; 3: 26)

When I arrived in Quebec City on January 10th in1990 to start my PhD studies, the town was completely white covered with snow and I went directly to the office of Professor Serge Kaliaguine at Laval University to introduce myself to him. After introductions with the other students, I spent my first week looking for a room around the university. Once I was familiar with my research topic and the laboratory, I sometimes visited the office of Professor Kaliaguine to discuss some challenges I was facing and we had long meetings only when I had enough experimental data to publish a scientific paper. On the other hand, when I assumed my role as a postdoctoral researcher at the Osaka National Institute, the leader of the research group, Professor Hiroyuki Kojima, came to the airport to welcome me and invited me for a Japanese dinner before taking me the furnished apartment that the research center rented for me. In order to have a welcoming start, a party was organized for me in a restaurant where all the members of the research group seemed very relaxed and happy talking to me.

However, when I started my work the next week, I was surprised noticing a very different behavior in the research center. First, nobody seemed to know me anymore. Secondly, researchers had always a serious face and very busy walking fast in the corridors of the research center. Thirdly, the "boss" is very important person in Japan and is treated almost as a God. In this perspective, Professor Kojima was always the first team member to arrive at work but the first to leave; no one should leave before him. When he left, he always said the same sentence "Shitsureishimashita (Sorry I am leaving before you)". When I started on the research program, Professor Kojima was supportive, and often asked me if I needed his help and we had group meetings almost every week to discuss the results and challenges of every member of the research team. Outside the workplace, Professor Kojima once invited me to have dinner with his family and came also to my home many times to share a coffee and discuss my research work. During the weekends, Professor Kojima also invited us to the research center to play football or ping pong with him. One week end, I had another plan but my Japanese colleague told me "when the boss invites you for any activity, it means that you have to go".

"Let there rise out of you a group of people inviting to all that is good, enjoining all that Islam orders one to do and forbidding all that Islam has forbidden. And it is they who are the successful" (Quran; 3:104)

The influence of managers on the efficiency of workflow at any level of the hierarchy, depends mainly on how they affect (soft skills) the employees under their supervision. Eight recognized leadership styles are evident in the literature, namely: (a) Democratic, (b) Autocratic, (c) Laissez-faire, (d) Strategic, (e) Transformational, (f) Transactional, (g) Bureaucratic and (h) Servant [30-33]. In addition to the style of leadership, the personality traits suggested for highly desirable managers are: (a) confidence (b) honesty (c) communication skills (d) empathy (e) optimism (f) encouragement (g) intuition (h) acting as a role model [34]. It's been widely found in research that managers who help employees under their supervision to succeed could also make them better leaders (Figure 9).

Figure 9: Helping Others Makes Better Leaders [35].

Mary Kay Ash reiterates "We need leaders who add value to the people and the organization they lead; who work for the benefit of others and not just for their own personal gain. Leaders who inspire and motivate, not intimidate and manipulate; who live with people to know their problems in order to solve them and who follow a moral compass that points in the right direction regardless of the trends" [36].

> *"And We made them leaders, guiding by Our command; and We revealed to them the doing of good deeds, performing the prayer, and the giving of charity. And of Us alone they were worshippers" (Quran; 21:73)*

According to the Noble Quran, leadership is a sacred position that can solve the problems of humanity and guide people to Allah (SWT). Prophet Mohamed (PBUH) exemplifies the teachings of Allah (SWT) in all areas of life. He models leadership distinctiveness as the greatest reformer and leader, and can be observed to exhibit the personification of morality, honesty, truthfulness, understanding of others, and enlightening effective commanding[37]. For example, in order to maximize the amount of workflow, a good leader should identify the positive and negative traits of each member of his team and make decisions based on them. In this aspect of leadership, one of the famous companions, Bilal ibn Rabah, had a very beautiful voice, and the Prophet (PBUH) being aware of this gift declared Bilal to be his official mu'adhin (one who calls Muslims to prayer). On the other hand, The Prophet (PBUH) refused to offer another distinguished companion, Abu Dharr al-Ghifari, an administrative responsibility because he lacked the required skills[38]. Based on the Noble Quran and teachings of the Prophet Mohamed (PBUH), Muslim managers should have the following attitudes in order to manage the workflows efficiently and lead people to the Eternal Path of Charity:

Muslim leaders should be obeyed by followers as Allah says "O you who believe! Obey Allah, and obey the Messenger

(Muhammad), and those of you who are in authority. And If you differ in anything amongst yourselves, refer it to Allah and His Messenger, if you believe in Allah and the Last Day: That is better, and more suitable for final determination" (Quran; 4:59).

At the same time, Muslim leaders should not show signs of superiority as Prophet Mohamed (PBUH) said ""Whoever has arrogance in his heart equal to an atom's weight shall not enter Paradise"[39].

Being a leader by remaining a servant, and maintaining humility, as Prophet Mohamed (PBUH) was always amongst his people: teaching, helping and guiding them. He never pursued comfort or a higher position over his people [40].

Muslim leaders should show empathy as Allah (SWT) says about Prophet Mohamed (PBUH) "Verily, there has come to you a Messenger (Muhammad) from amongst yourselves. It grieves him that you should receive any injury or difficulty. He is anxious over you, for the believers, he is full of pity, kind and merciful." (Quran; 9: 128).

Islam promotes shared responsibility as Prophet Mohamed (PBUH) said, "Every one of you is a shepherd and is responsible for his flock"[41].

Muslim leaders should also be approachable as mentioned in the Quran: "And by mercy from Allah, you (Muhammad) dealt with them gently. And had you been severe and harsh-hearted, they would have broken away from about you; so, pass over (their faults) and ask Allah forgiveness for them" (Quran; 3:159).

Muslim leaders are also advised to share decisions-making with employees as indicated in this Quranic verse "And consult them in the affairs" (Quran; 3.159).

"Then think of the Day We shall summon every community with its leader. Those who are given their Record in their right hand shall read the Record of their deeds and shall not be wronged a whit." (Quran; 17:71)

Leadership in Islam is an onerous responsibility and a divine duty not everyone is qualified for. For example, it has been reported on the authority of 'Abd al-Rahman b. Samura who said: The Prophet (PBUH) said to me: 'Abd al-Rahman, do not ask for a position of authority, for if you are granted this position as a result of your asking for it, you will be left alone (without God's help to discharge the responsibilities attendant thereon), and it you are granted it without making any request for it, you will be helped (by God in the discharge of your duties)[42]. Therefore, since unfair attitudes of managers may prevent employees to self-purifying their soul in the Eternal Path of Charity, Allah (SWT) warns Muslim leaders

> *"Surely Allah enjoins justice, kindness and the doing of good to kith and kin, and forbids all that is shameful, evil and oppressive. He exhorts you so that you may be mindful"* (Quran; 16:90).

Consumerism and Warnings from The Merciful (SWT)

"As to those who believe and work righteousness, verily We shall not suffer to perish the reward of any who do a (single) righteous deed" (Quran; 18:30)

As I arrived in New York City in early October of 1980 to start my graduate studies in the USA, the Christmas celebration season of that year was particularly exciting. Being a resident at International House, I saw for the first time a widely diverse multi-cultural groups of students talking happily to each other. I still remember that evening when I went with my Algerian friend Amr to contemplate for the first time the Christmas decorations in Midtown Manhattan. While having a pizza near the ice rink of the Rockefeller center, we were enjoying looking at happy people skating under the Christmas tree and, at the same time, I was watching the well-dressed ladies and gentlemen leaving the tall buildings around the center and walking fast in the endless avenues of Manhattan. After a while, we decided to follow the lively crowd until Macy's department store. From the main door, we could hear soft Christmas songs welcoming customers. Inside the store, employees looked very excited to help clients buy different types of gifts. On our way back to International House, there was a lot of loud music on Broadway as we met black beggars happily dancing as they received food and money from people leaving the shopping centers. When we arrived at International House, many of the students were having a late dinner together and talking cheerfully like family members around the Christmas tree.

"And man has been created weak (lacking firmness to control his vain desires and passions)" (Quran; 4:28)

In general, striving to satisfy physiological needs, security, connection to other human beings, esteem and reaching one's full potential are the driving forces behind corresponding social and professional activities. In order to create the same picture of the natural flows in the water cycle, the displacements of people driving on a daily basis in the highways and streets of the cities are described in this book as "social flows". However, in contradiction with the fact that flows in nature obey the two divine laws of charity, human beings follow individual paths to fulfill their specific needs.

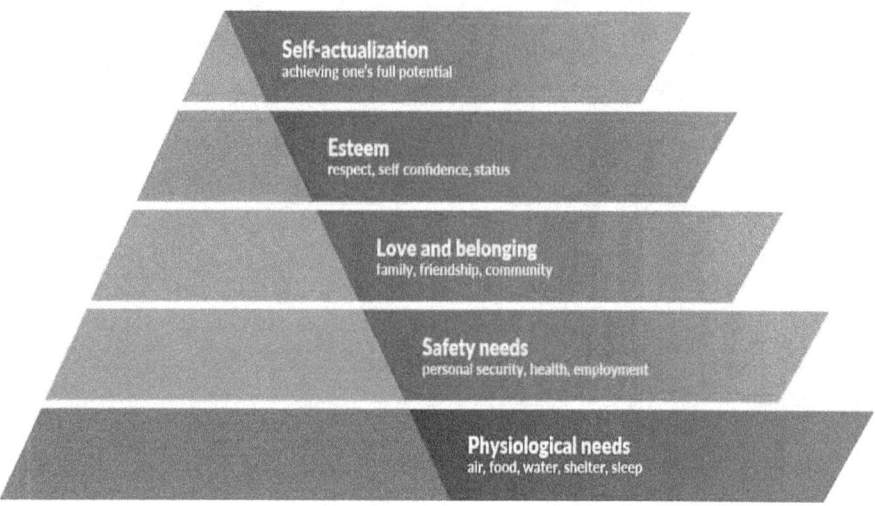

Figure 10: Maslow's Hierarchy of Needs[43]

For example, as shown in Figure 10, in terms of esteem, students go through a "social flow of education" to prepare for their career. In a quest to achieve security in life, people are part of the "social flow of professional activities". To meet their physiological needs, people follow the "social flow of consumption" that leads them to markets and shopping centers. People also spend time with family members, friends and neighbors for the "social flow of love and belonging". Finally, according to "self-actualizing", individuals who are highly creative demonstrate a desire to resolve dichotomies inherent in ultimate contradictions, such as life versus death and freedom versus determinism[44].

In order to apply the 2nd universal law of dynamic systems (Equation 3) for "social flows", people are considered to have a specific motivation for getting in their car to drive in order to accomplish a desired activity. At the same time, an obstacle or an event could make them cancel the activity or slow down their displacement. For example, bad weather is an obstacle for anyone who is due to go to the workplace. The application of the 2nd universal law of dynamic systems (Equation 3) for social flows of any social or professional activity could then be represented as:

$$Social\ flow\ \propto\ \frac{(Motivation\ )}{(Obstacle\ )}$$

Equation (12)

Because consumption is closely related to selfishness and opposite concept to charity, this social activity and its consequences are investigated in this chapter of the book. In this social flow, people are therefore motivated to go to markets or shopping centers to spend their money in order to buy the needed goods, defined as "utility". On the other hand, the amount of money spent during their shopping depends on personal income. In general, when income is lower, less spending occurs. Therefore, the personal income could be seen as a "conductor" for shopping and, by consequence, the inverse of income could be interpreted as the resistance to shopping. Finally, for any shopping activity, the flow of consumption (FC_1) could be qualitatively described as[45]:

$$Flow\ of\ Consumption\ (FC_1) \propto \frac{Utility}{\left(\dfrac{1}{income}\right)}$$

Equation (13)

"O children of Adam, take your adornment while praying, and eat and drink, but waste not by extravagance. Certainly, He likes not those who commit extravagance." (Quran; 7:31)

Gross Domestic Product (GDP) is defined as the broadest quantitative measure of a nation's total economic activity and a consumer economy describes an economy driven by consumer spending as a percentage of its GDP. For example, in the USA, the consumer spending accounts for up to 68% of GDP[46]. The consumption of goods certainly has a positive effect on the global economic growth, but today's marketing is responsible for the accelerated increase in the world's overconsumption of goods. For example, in order to compete in this "consumption-based economy", companies started to focus on people using advertisements for their products as a "tactic" to influence their mind to push them to spend more money in their shops. Therefore, by influencing the consumers' minds to become impulse buyers instead of buying only what they need (utility), marketing increases the driving force for buying and by consequence the flow of consumption will become the flow of overconsumption[45]:

$$Flow\ of\ overconsumption\ (FC_2) \propto \frac{(Utility + Marketing)}{\left(\frac{1}{income}\right)}$$

Equation (14)

"Give to the near of kin his due, and also to the needy and the wayfarer. Do not squander your wealth wastefully, for those who squander wastefully are Satan's brothers, and Satan is ever ungrateful to his Lord" (Quran; 17: 26-27)

Moreover, in order to encourage the acquisition of more goods and services, the other way to make costumers spend more money is to boost their income in order to decrease the resistance for spending. Since they cannot increase the income, banks and companies introduced the Credit Card to offer loans as artificial incomes to take even more money from the pocket of customers. For example, according to a survey in 2017, Americans' total credit card debt reached $927 billion, which is more than a 5% increase from the year 2106[47]. Unfortunately, consumerism is intensifying like a plague in today's way of life where people behave more like guided spending engines whose lifestyles are centered on malls, sales, and new offers. For example, some statistics show that we wear 20% of our clothes 80% of the time. That means that many of us have closets full of clothes that we no longer like or no longer fit us properly[48]. The corresponding flow of consumerism could be qualitatively described as[45]:

$$Flow\ of\ consumerism\ (FC_3) \propto \frac{Utility\ +\ Marketing}{\left(\dfrac{1}{income\ +\ Loan}\right)}$$

Equation (15)

In conclusion, after being influenced by marketing to buy more than is needed, it's common to become trapped in a debt cycle of repaying companies credit debt for goods which may even have become worn or worthless.

> "Know well that the life of this world is merely sport and diversion and adornment and an object of your boasting with one another, and a rivalry in the multiplication of riches and children. Its likeness is that of rain: when it produces vegetation it delights the tillers. But then it withers and you see it turn yellow, and then it crumbles away. In the Hereafter there is (either) grievous chastisement (or) forgiveness from Allah and (His) good pleasure. The life of this world is nothing but delusion..." (Quran; 57:20)

Consumerism, enhanced by marketing and loans, could be explained by the fact that the goal of companies and banks is always to maximize their profits in order to stay competitive. This selfish behavior is in concordance with Maslow's theory (Figure 10) which states that human beings are mainly motivated by activities that only benefit them. However, in contradiction with the 1st divine law of charity imposed by Allah (SWT) on the whole universe, the money in the "social flow of consumerism" flows from the poor consumers to the much richer companies and banks. Therefore, this deviation from the Quranic verse "Indeed we have sent Our Messengers with clear proof, and revealed with them the Scripture and the balance that mankind may keep justice" (Quran; 57:25), is the main source of international injustice, the increasing gap between poor and rich, the rise of poverty worldwide, global warming, the human emigration flows to rich countries, crimes and wars.

"Yet no sooner than they saw some trading or amusement, they flocked to it and left you standing by yourself. Tell them: That which is with Allah is far better than amusement and trading. Allah is the Best Provider of sustenance." (Quran; 62:11)

For example, the reason of consumerism is the common belief that we are buying comfort and pleasure and ultimately happiness. The sad reality is that the search for comfort and pleasures has serious consequences for humanity such as anxiety, depression and loneliness of the soul. For example, in the research paper, "The High Price of Materialism"[49], the authors show that people who manage their lives around extrinsic goals such as product acquisition, experience greater unhappiness in relationships, poorer moods and more psychological problems. Furthering this findings, research psychologist Brock Bastian argues that a willingness to experience discomfort is crucial to our pursuit of genuine happiness, and that our efforts to escape unpleasantness or seek out only the positive in fact weaken us in managing life's inevitable difficulties[50]. Closer to us, Prophet Mohamed (PBUH) warns us about the consequences of being attached to material possessions: "Be happy, and hope for what will please you. By God, I am not afraid that you will be poor, but I fear that worldly wealth will be bestowed upon you as it was bestowed upon those who lived before you. So, you will compete amongst yourselves for it, as they competed for it and it will destroy you as it did them[51].

"And do not do mischief on the earth after it has been set in order." (Quran; 7:56)

Besides hurting our well being, there is every day a new proof of our unmanageable effect on the environment as all signs are indicating to human activity is driving the Earth to the edge.

Moreover, according to this Quranic verse, the increasing amount of carbon dioxide emissions caused mainly by consumerism is disrupting the chemical balance imposed by Allah (SWT) on the atmospheric air. As a consequence, an increased amount of energy (heat) striking the earth from the sun is being trapped in the atmosphere and not radiated out into space. The resulting global warming is causing natural disasters (Figure 11) because it becomes more difficult for the environment to find a new balance which could also damage the beauty and Blessings of every season. Furthermore, based on this Quranic verse: "Evil has appeared on land and sea because of what the hands of men have earned. He may make them taste a part of that which they have done, in order that they may return." (Quran; 30:41), scientists at the COP 21 have warned us that the outcomes of global warming include increased risk of drought and increased intensity of storms, including tropical cyclones with higher wind speeds, a wetter Asian monsoon, and, possibly, more intense mid-latitude storms[52].

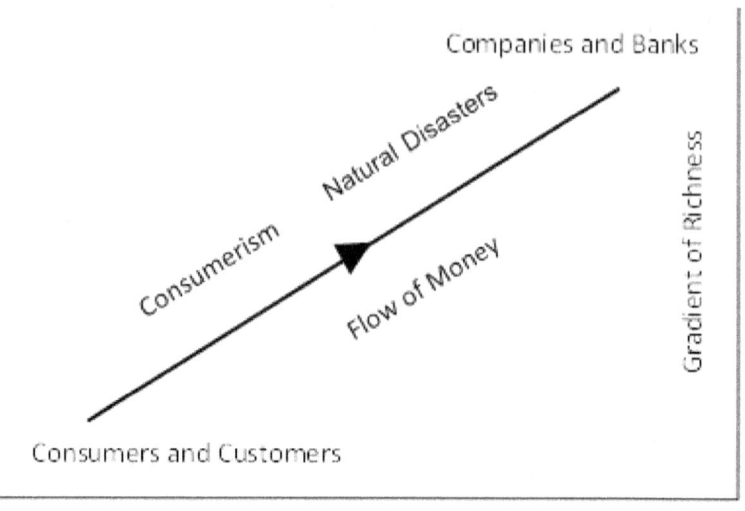

Figure 11: Consumerism and Natural Disasters

"Tell them, (O Prophet): "If your fathers and your sons and your brothers and your wives and your tribe and the riches you have acquired and the commerce of which you fear a slackening, and the dwellings that you love, if they are dearer to you than Allah and His Messenger and striving in His cause, then wait until Allah brings about His decree. Allah does not guide the evil-doing folk." (Quran; 9:24)

Looking for solutions to global warming, the IPCC's report indicates that lifestyle and behavioral changes could reduce energy demand by up to 20% in the short term and by up to 50% of present levels by mid-century[53]. As a consequence, future events on the planet seem to depend more on our daily actions and attitudes than on the advance in technologies. Indeed, since Allah (SWT) loves all His creatures, His Mercy will not allow us to continue to violate His divine laws of charity and preserve our lifestyle based on pleasures and consumption that could lead us to great misfortune. Therefore, finding technical solutions to carbon dioxide emissions will never be the solution. Based on this Quranic verse, the increase of intensity of the natural disasters could just be a sign and warning from Allah (SWT) to humanity through nature in order to make us reconsider our lifestyle. This is now supported by the recent coronavirus pandemic that could be another global warning sign from The Merciful (SWT) to force humanity to change the life style based on consumerism. Indeed, the coronavirus pandemic has obliged countries around the world to scale down economic activities. As a positive result, the global carbon dioxide emissions have significantly decreased[54].

"And I did not create the jinn and mankind except to worship Me" (Quran; 51:56)

Allah (SWT) created us as an organization with a hierarchy. As leaders, the brain and the heart are located at the top of the hierarchy. As they are vital both of them are protected respectively by the skull and the thorax. On the other hand, the parts of our body related to our physiological needs are located in the lower part and are not protected. The brain and the heart are therefore supposed to guide our actions and manage our emotions that could help us make the right decisions to positively affect the future events of our planet. Therefore, according to this Quranic verse, the wisdom that will save humanity from more misfortunes is to obey the divine laws of charity of the Merciful (SWT) who created us and certainly knows what is best for His creatures. In this perspective, in order to shift from consumerism to charity-based societies, some people are already adopting "minimalist" lifestyles[48]. The most important benefits of this new way of life are reducing waste to help the environment, decreasing global carbon dioxide emissions and saving money and time used for excess consumption to worship Allah (SWT) by helping others during charity-based activities. Finally, about the discomfort of natural disasters and the recent coronavirus pandemic, "The Merciful" (SWT) says

> "Verily, along with every hardship is relief. So, when you have finished your occupation, devote yourself to Allah's worship. And to your Lord (Alone) turn your intentions and hopes" (Quran; 94: 6-8).

Islam-based Educational Model

"And whosoever fears Allah and keeps his duty to Him, He will make a way for him to get out from every difficulty. And He will provide him from sources he never could imagine. And whosoever puts his trust in Allah the He will suffice him." (Quran; 65:2-3)

I started my undergraduate studies at the Algerian Petroleum Institute in September of 1975. I was an average student who enjoyed learning and was not overly worried about grades. At the end of the fourth academic year, three students with the best GPA were selected by the school to pursue their graduate studies at the United States of America. To complete the theoretical part of the studies, the fifth year was a technical training program where students went on work placement for a period of nine months in different chemical plants to study the processes and return to the university to present their project in front of a panel. When I arrived in the LPG plant in the city of Arzew, located in the western part of Algeria, I learned that the plant had been shut down few days ago because of a technical problem related to the flare. Knowing that it would take many months to solve the problem and start the plant again, the manager of the gas plant advised me to join the technical team and learn from the design of the new flare. At the end of the work placement, I returned to the institute to present my technical project to a panel. Unlike other students who presented mainly the description of the chemical processes of their corresponding industrial plants, my presentation was based on difficult design calculations of the flare that I learned from the engineers of the LPG plant. The panel was surprised by the high quality of my presentation and awarded the highest grade. As a result, I got the second-best GPA of the promotion and Professor Costas Gogos, from Stevens Institute of Technology (NJ, USA) offered me a scholarship to continue my graduate studies. Looking back at this special event of my life and with my current understanding of Islam, I know now that, without being among the best students of the class, "The Opener" (SWT) created that "coincidence" of the technical problem in the chemical plant that helped me do an excellent presentation and opened the door for me to pursue my graduate studies in the United States of America.

"They said. "Glory to You! We have no knowledge except what You taught us. You, only You, are All-Knowing, All-Wise" (Quran; 2:32)

The relationship between knowledge and our daily actions is a key topic in psychology and, according to Joachim Funke, it is not possible to act without knowledge[55]. However, every new-born baby has the instinct to latch on and suck milk rhythmically from the breast of their mother and that instinctive action needs knowledge, so Who gave them this knowledge in order to be able to live? The other example that shows that Allah (SWT) is the One who teaches us everything is in the Quranic verse "And among you there is he who is brought back to the miserable age, so he knows nothing after having known" (Quran; 22:5). This state of forgetting even the names and faces of family members is known as the Alzheimer's disease, which usually affects people over sixty-five years of age. In this perspective, by His beautiful Names "The Omniscient" and "The Illuminator", Allah (SWT) is therefore the Absolute Teacher and the Absolute Guide of humanity as mentioned in the Quranic verse "And Allah taught Adam all the names" (Quran; 2:31).

> "Indeed, Allah conferred a great favor on the believers when He sent among them a Messenger from among themselves, reciting to them His verses (the Quran) and purifying them and instructing them the Book (Quran) and wisdom (Sunnah), while before that they had been in manifest error." (Quran; 3:164)

The advent of the Noble Quran in the seventh century was quite revolutionary for the predominantly illiterate Arabian society. Since the Noble Quran is the book of Allah (SWT) and needed to be organically interacted with by means of reading and reciting its words, reading and writing for the purpose of accessing the full blessings of the Noble Quran was an aspiration for most Muslims. Thus, education in Islam unequivocally derived its origins from a symbiotic relationship with religious instruction. Moreover, Islam has, from its inception, placed a high premium on education and has enjoyed a long and rich intellectual tradition. In fact, Islamic education is uniquely different from other types of educational theory and practice largely because of the all-encompassing influence of the Noble Quran. For example, the importance of education is repeatedly emphasized in the Noble Quran with frequent injunctions, such as "God will exalt those of you who believe and those who have knowledge to high degrees" (Quran; 58:11), "O my Lord! Increase me in knowledge" (Quran; 20:114), and "As God has taught him, so let him write" (Quran; 2:282). Such Quranic verses provide a forceful stimulus for the Islamic community to strive for education and learning. The most important is that the conception of knowledge (Al-Ilm) in Islam is the Guiding Light (Huda) separating right from wrong (Al furqan). Therefore, in the same way, the sun brings light to our eyes to see the world around us, Al-Ilm is the source of guidance to see the Truth.

On a last note, the sacred position of knowledge in Islam is also proven by the fact that the word "science" and its derivations appear 779 times (averaging 7 times a chapter) in the Noble Quran. This is the second position after the word "Allah"[56]. Finally, the importance of seeking knowledge in Islam is also shown by the fact that the first Quranic verse sent to Prophet Muhammad (PBUH) by Allah (SWT) through Angel Gabriel started with "Read! In the Name of your Lord Who has created all that exists" (Quran; 96:1).

"Are those who know equal to those who do not know?"
Only those endowed with understanding take heed" (Quran; 39:9)

Since education is the key to solve social and technical problems the world is facing today, this book proposes an Islam-based educational model that includes the teaching methods of Prophet Muhammad (PBUH). First, similar to this book, in order to teach natural and social sciences under the umbrella of the Divine Science, Quranic verses and the Prophet (PBUH)'s sayings could be integrated in the corresponding chapters of the textbooks and the teaching material. Therefore, teachers should not only have the expertise in their field of science but also a good knowledge of the

Noble Quran and The Prophet (PBUH)'s sayings. The final goal of this Islam-based educational model is that the objectives of educational systems and scientific research will not be dictated by rich individuals and companies who are continuously looking for personal profits but to serve all humanity in order to solve local and global problems. Moreover, new scientific knowledge will be developed as a means to search for the Truth that brings us closer to Allah (SWT). Finally, graduate students will be more prepared and willing to please Allah (SWT) by fulfilling their divine duties in their future workplaces and add the daily activities as good deeds in the Eternal Path of charity.

"And you are certainly on the most exalted standard of moral excellence" (Quran; 68:4)

Regarding the utilization of the teaching methods of Prophet Muhammad (PBUH) in an Islam-based educational system, The Prophet (PBUH) adopted a distinctive approach to teach his followers and companions the basics and concepts of Islam, which comes from divine revelation. His teachings covered all aspects of life, work, living and human dealings, which are suitable everywhere and anytime. First, in order to deal properly with different types of people, The Prophet (PBUH) said Allah (SWT) created Adam from the grip of taking possession from all over the globe, came to the sons of Adam on earth came to them as much as the white, red and black, and between it, malignant, good, sadness and in between. This means that humans are different as they belong to their father who created from clay made of earth sands. Hence each individual (or groups) may need specific dealing treatments[57]. Secondly, regarding the openness to other communities, the Prophet (PBUH) encouraged his followers to be open on other communities in order to know their customs, morals and behaviors. For example, the prophet (PBUH) asked one of his followers to learn Hebrew to be the prophet translator who could understand the Jews tribes' messages and reply to them in Hebrew[57].

"Surely there was a good example for you in the Messenger of Allah, for all those who look forward to Allah and the Last Day and remember Allah much" (Quran; 33:21)

Thirdly, in order to be able to fully transmit his divine message to educate people around him, Prophet Muhammad (PBUH) addressed first the hearts to become the beloved one in order to inspire his followers to listen to his message[58]. Fourthly, in order to maximize the effects of his message that could permanently transform the behaviour of people, he used a type of speech that made his followers think during his educational methods, mainly based on active learning and analogies[58-59]. The objective of using analogies was to enhance the imagination and curiosity of the listeners. Fifthly, The Prophet (PBUH) utilized wondering and interrogative while teaching his followers, this style is one of the important and influential methods in the field of education that creates positive interaction between student and teacher. The objective to utilize the interrogative question as an educational style with his followers is to stimulate their minds for thinking and understanding. These are some examples of his teaching strategies: (1) the Prophet (PBUH) asked his companions, "What would be the situation of someone who has a river at his door and every day, five times a day, he comes out and he takes a bath in that river? At the end of the day would he have any dirt on himself?" They responded, "There would be no dirt on him, O RasulAllah." Then the Prophet said, "Similarly there are the five prayers cleansing the person in this way; (2) As the Prophet (PBUH) used this analogy to explain a topic verbally, he also used illustration to make a point graphically. In this context, the Prophet drew a straight line through the sand and then drew lines to the right and lines to the left of the first line. Then while people were looking attentively at the drawing, he recited the Quranic verse "And verily, this (Allah' commandments) is My Straight Path, so follow it, and follow not (other) paths, for they will separate you away from His Path" (Quran; 6:153); (3) On other occasions, he illustrated his point using his hand as once he said, "I and the one who takes care of the orphans are in paradise, like this (as he was speaking, he interlaced his fingers); (4) His teaching was also based on living experiences as opportunity to instruct. For example, The Prophet (PBUH) once was with some companions to prepare food, he asked them to slaughter a sheep. One companion said he would do that, another said he would skin it, and a third said he would cook it. Then the Messenger of Allah (SWT) replied, "I will collect wood for the fire." They said, "No, we will do that work for you." The Prophet (PBUH) answered, "I know that you can do it for me, but Allah (SWT) hates to see a servant of his privileged above others." And the Prophet went and collected firewood; (5) The Prophet at times would readdress a question to a subject that is more significant and instructive. Once a Bedouin asked the Prophet (PBUH): "When is the hour?" [The Day of Judgment]. The Prophet (PBUH) said, "What have you prepared for that final hour?" The Bedouin said, "I haven't prepared a lot of salah (good deeds) and I haven't prepared a lot of zakah (charity) but I am preparing one thing which is my love for Allah (SWT) and His messenger." The Prophet (PBUH) replied: "You will be with who you love"[59].

"Bring me ingots of iron." Then after he had filled up the space between the two mountain-sides, he said: "(Light a fire) and ply bellows." When he had made it (red like) fire, he said: "Bring me molten copper which I may pour on it." (Quran; 18:96)

Nowadays, each type of profession has a needed level of Knowledge, Skills, and Abilities (KSA) that are essential for success on the job. KSA is most often used to define the requirements of a job opening and compare applicants when making a final choice. First, we are all born with some talents since some people have a body suitable for certain sports, others are especially skilled at their hands, some are really good in connecting with people, and others are brilliant at school. This innate ability could be explained by the fact that people can study at university the techniques of negotiation by acquiring knowledge about it and practicing the skills it requires. On the other hand, few are brilliant negotiators because they have the inborn attitude and soft skill to persuade.

However, if we are born with an innate ability but don't improve it, it's unlikely that it will have an influence on our professional life. It requires seeking the necessary knowledge and skills to be able to apply the inborn ability as a powerful advantage for a future job. For this purpose, teachers are the source of knowledge and skills in the different departments of social and natural sciences. Indeed, their teaching strategies and conduct will affect the behaviour of the graduate students during their future professional activities. In order to apply this Islam based educational model in Muslim countries, as the Prophet (PBUH) considered the individual differences while dealing with people, the most suitable educational system is the one that focuses on the students in order to give them the opportunity to learn what aligns with their own innate abilities the best. For instance, based on creativity, originality, and responsibility during the learning experience, the key advantage of "student-centered" learning (SCL) is that the teacher gives to the students an opportunity to learn and apply concepts on their own with minimal teacher intervention and supervision[60]. In other words, SCL aims to develop learner autonomy and independence and the teacher's role inside the classroom is like a "coach" who facilitates learning. Moreover, SCL focuses on skills and practices that enable lifelong learning and independent problem-solving. Therefore, as students will put energy into what they are naturally passionate about, they will acquire the expertise and skills to develop their innate ability[60].

In addition, in order to help students absorb the requisite amount of knowledge and skills that correspond to their innate aptitude, Muslim teachers should learn from the methods by which The Prophet (PBUH) taught his companions. For instance, as a teacher at the Higher Colleges of Technology (UAE), I realized that students in engineering departments link an equation learned in a course as a unique theory specific to the subject and fail to realize that it is part of a more universal principle that can be applied to a wide variety of natural phenomena. For this reason, they are able to use formulas related to the theory perfectly, but fail to visualize the basic concepts hidden behind the applications. Without having the ability to create a bridge between the theory and its applications, students will often have misconceptions and learning difficulties. On the other hand, these students will become engineers and need critical and creative thinking to solve future technical problems or innovate a new process. Therefore, teaching thinking skills is far more important than just giving information. So, what teaching strategies can engage students in thinking and to be deeply involved in learning? (1) As The Prophet (PBUH) taught us, a positive mindset is vital to make students to be open to thinking: Indeed literature has shown that effective teachers have succeeded in making students feel happy about learning and make them more interested by increasing their intrinsic motivation[61] (2) As the Prophet (PBUH) used living experiences as opportunity to instruct , it was also found that students in an actively taught class get more engaged in learning and develop more skills because they have more autonomy to learn and they get more involved in thinking during the practical activities[61]. (3) Finally, as used by the Prophet (PBUH), analogies are very powerful tool to visualize the theory. Indeed, the use of an analog concept could help students develop images in their minds in order to visualize the physical phenomena behind each theoretical formula. The use of analogies could therefore help students have more knowledge and skills because of their higher order of thinking[62].

As an example, to demonstrate the beneficial effects of the use of analogies and active learning strategies on the learning process, the 2nd universal law of dynamic systems (Equation 3) is utilized in this book to present a mathematical model in order to quantify the amount of knowledge and skills acquired by students (flow of knowledge and skills). First, it is assumed that the student's innate abilities are represented by the Cumulative Grade point Average (CGPA). Since students with higher CGPA learn faster, the "Resistance" to the learning process is therefore equal to the inverse of the Cumulative Grade Point Average (1/CGPA). The following qualitative equation describes the amount of knowledge and skills acquired by students[61]:

$$Flow\ of\ (knowledge + skills) \propto \frac{Motivation\ of\ student}{\left(\frac{1}{CGPA}\right)}$$

Equation (16)

If the learned knowledge and skills could be approximately represented by the Final Grade Point (FGP) which is assumed to be a direct measure of student performance and introducing a correction factor ($\propto$), the Dadach Motivation Factor (DMF) of students is introduced [61]:

$$FGP = (DMF).(\alpha).(CGPA)$$

Equation (17)

Based on Equation (17), for any innate ability (CGPA) of students to learn, the teaching strategies that increase the intrinsic motivation (DMF) of students will be able to enhance the amount of information acquired by each student by unlocking (her/his) full inborn potential. It will then result in the maximum possible amount of knowledge obtained in the course and highest ability to master the needed skills for their future job. Indeed, my recent academic research show that the teaching strategies used by Prophet Muhammad (PBUH) have the potential to enhance the motivation and performance of students[61-62]. Finally, because they can use their full inborn ability complete with the needed knowledge and skills, the intrinsically motivated students will be equipped with the highest possible technical hard skills (KSA= Knowledge, Skills, Ability) to fully fulfill their divine duties to enhance the workflows in their future workplaces.

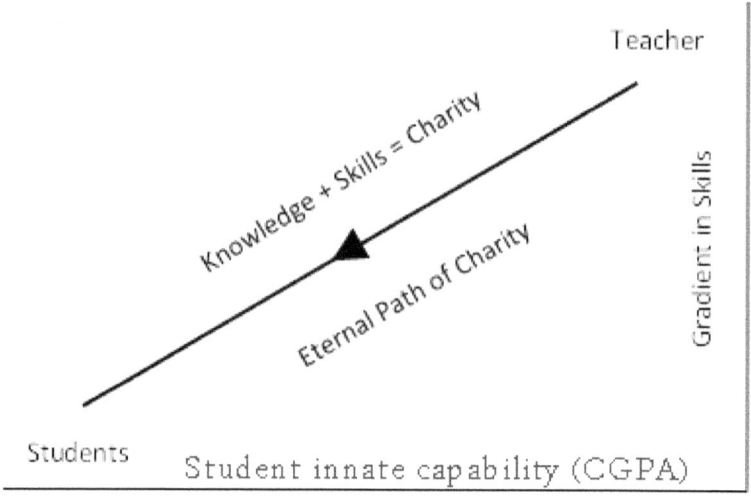

Figure 12: Eternal Path of Charity in Classrooms

Teachers have a very high status in Islam as Prophet Muhammad (PBUH) said: "The virtue of the scholar over the worshiper is like my virtue over the least of you. Verily, Allah, his angels, the inhabitants of the heavens and earth, even the ant in his hole and the fish, send blessings upon the one who teaches people what is good."[63]. Therefore, since their intention is to please Allah (SWT) (1st divine law of charity) by helping students to succeed, Muslim educators will self-purify their soul in the Eternal Path of Charity (Figure 12) and add the flow of knowledge and skills as good deeds (2nd divine law of charity).

On a last note, similar to the fact that the Prophet encouraged his followers to be open on other nations in order to know their customs, morals and behaviors, schools and universities in Muslim countries could have departments of languages and cultures in order to encourage students to learn some languages and know different cultures in order to be able to communicate with people around the planet to deliver the message of Islam with wisdom and peacefully.

The Eternal Spring

"And give glad tidings to those who believe and do righteous good deeds that for them, will be gardens under which rivers flow (Paradise). Every time they will be provided with a fruit therefrom, they will say 'This is what we were provided with before.' And they will be given things in resemblance and they shall have therein purified wives and they will abide therein forever." (Quran; 2:25)

My strongest feeling of spring was during the year of 1995 in the small town of Ikeda near Osaka city (Japan). Before spring and on my way to the research center, I became accustomed to seeing Japanese with very serious faces walking fast in the streets. However, by the middle of March, I realized that people started to look happier and the walk became more relaxed. They seemed to be in tune with the pink color appearing in the trees and the warm weather of spring. During the first week of April, spring had arrived in full over Ikeda. Some cherry trees of the town had light pink to white blossoms and other cherry trees with dark pink, yellow or green blossoms. The streets became livelier and many people and companies organized parties the parks. One day, I went with my boss and all the research team to relax in a park. I was surprised to see for the first time the shy Japanese of all ages singing and dancing to celebrate under the pink cherry trees. Some people were also taking photographs of trees or individual flowers and others were smelling them deeply. I also met a few people reciting a Japanese poetry about Hanami (Cherry Blossoms) called "haiku".

By the end of May, the trees started to lose their beautiful leaves as the light falling rain seemed also to wash away the resident's joy. Faces in the streets became serious again like the naked trees of the parks. During that period, the streets of the quiet town were covered with pink petals announcing the hot and very humid season of summer.

"By the soul and Him Who perfected him in proportion, then He showed him what is wrong for him and what is right it for him. Indeed, he succeeded who purifies his own self and he fails who corrupts his own self." (Quran; 91:7-10)

In concordance with this Quranic verse, Prophet Muhammad (PBUH) made an analogy in the following hadith (saying) "The parable of the five prayers is that of a river running at our door in which we self-purify ourselves five times a day"[64]. Considering the time spent in one day for prayers to Allah (SWT) as a charity for Him, my understanding is that the rivers described in this saying could be the Eternal Path of Charity that purifies our soul. Indeed, with every single act of goodness, we feel the Nearness and the Mercy of Allah (SWT) as the Noble Quran says "Surely Allah's Mercy is ever near to the good-doers" (Quran; 7:56). Therefore, similar to the lovely nature after the Cyclic Flow of Charity, the divine reward of helping others is certainly a feeling of spring. In this topic, Prophet Mohammad (PBUH) added: "True enrichment does not come through possessing a lot of wealth, but true enrichment is the enrichment of the soul"[65]. This saying of The Prophet (PBUH) is now supported scientifically, by MRI scans which demonstrate a "warm-glow effect" in the reward centers of the brain in certain situations. Research was conducted in the form of experiments in which a group of people were given money, with half of them instructed to spend it on themselves and the other half required to spend it on other people. Contrary to their own expectations, the half who spent the money on others were shown to consistently get more pleasure out of the experience than their non-altruistic colleagues[66].

"The description of Paradise which the pious have been promised in it are rivers of water the taste and smell of which are not changed, rivers of milk of which the taste never changes, and rivers of wine delicious to those who drink, and rivers of clear and pure honey; therein for them is every kind of fruit and forgiveness from their Lord." (Quran; 47:15)

Besides the unseen garden of feeling the Mercy of Allah (SWT) in the Eternal Path of Charity, eternal gardens with flowing rivers are the last destination for the soul of the believers who please Allah (SWT) by helping people, animals and plants during their social and professional activities. This is supported by this Quranic verse "Therein they will cry: O Lord Brings us out, we shall do righteous good deeds not the evil deeds that we used to do." (Quran; 35:37). Indeed, the wrongdoers will cry and beg Allah (SWT) to get them out of Fire and bring them back to life to do good deeds. Even if each pillar of Islam is considered as a good deed to Allah (SWT), my understanding is that the good deeds mentioned in this Quranic verse are more about our divine duties of charity by helping others. This could therefore confirm that worshipping Allah (SWT) with our good actions and interactions with people, animals and plants during our social and professional activities could be much appreciated from Allah (SWT) and therefore our best path to the Eternal Spring. To the questions: Is the Eternal Path of Charity in this life the hidden Flowing Rivers of Paradise? Indeed, following Al Fitrah, it seems like good deeds bring us closer to the Gardens of Paradise and our soul feel happy. Therefore, is Paradise around us but unseen because our soul is in the jail of the senses of our body? A reminder that the Arabic word for Paradise is "Jannah" which means "to cover or hide something." Heaven, therefore, is a place that is unseen to us.

Concluding Remarks

"Surely those who believe (in the truths revealed in the Book) and do righteous deeds their Lord will guide them aright because of their faith. Rivers shall flow beneath them in the Gardens of Bliss. Their cry in it will be: 'Glory be to You, Our Lord!', and their greeting: 'Peace!'; and their cry will always end with: 'All praise be to Allah, the Lord of the universe" (Quran; 10, 9-10)

With His Infinite Love, Allah (SWT) created us to live eternally and happily in Paradise and this short life is only for the divine test. To explain this, The Prophet (PBUH) said: "Allah said, "I have prepared for My righteous slaves as no eye has ever seen, nor an ear has ever heard nor a human heart can ever think of[67]. The love and mercy Allah (SWT) demonstrates for human beings can be easily understood by reading the Noble Quran. Indeed, all chapters except one begin with: "In the name of Allah, Al-Rahman, Al-Raheem". Moreover, His Beautiful Names: "The Acceptor of Repentance"; "The Compassionate"; "The Loving One"; "The Forbearing One"; "The Most Gracious"; "The Most Merciful"; "The Source of Goodness"; "The Most Generous" and "The Bestower" indicate that He (SWT) is characterized by mercy, goodness and generosity.

"Say [O Prophet], 'If you do love Allah, follow me; Allah shall love you…" (Quran; 3: 31)

A distinguishing feature of believers is that Allah (SWT) loves them and they love Him. As Allah (SWT) says "O you who have believed, whoever of you should revert from his religion – Allah will bring forth [in place of them] a people He will love and who will love Him [who are] humble toward the believers, powerful against the disbelievers…" (Quran; 5: 54). Therefore, believers are those who love Allah (SWT) above all else. This is highlighted in this Quranic verse "Yet there are people who make others as God's equals, loving them as only God should be loved. But those who have faith love God more than all else…" (Quran; 2:165). Moreover, loving, caring for, supporting and nurturing people, animals and plants because they are all creations of Allah (SWT) is one of the strongest bonds of faith, and is one of the most important tenets on which Muslim society is based. In this topic, Prophet Muhammad (PBUH) said "Whoever loves for the sake of Allah, hates for the sake of Allah, gives for the sake of Allah, and withholds for the sake of Allah has perfected the faith."[68].

"As for those who believe and act righteously, their Lord shall admit them to His Mercy. That indeed is the manifest triumph." (Quran; 45:30)

I tried in this book to learn about the divine commandment that was meant for both the universe and humanity. The first connection that I could make is that both the universe and human beings are created to be in constant movement, which means dynamic and imbalanced systems. I understood that nature is imbalanced in energy because the sun does not equally warm up the different regions of earth. As for humanity, the inequity is due to the fact that Allah (SWT) created us within a "gradient" of wealth including finances, material elements, health, appearance, intelligence to learn and the ability to master different skills.

The most important lesson learned is that Allah (SWT) used nature as a universal school in order to show us that His science is based on charity. Based on the two Quranic verses (55:7 and 15:21) used to perceive the divine science and a spiritual view of movements in nature, I came also to understand that Allah (SWT) installs balance between the different regions of earth. To perceive this divine command, this book introduces two divine laws of charity of the divine science to try to explain how Allah (SWT) creates justice between the rich and the poor and install harmony in the universe.

For the same purpose, the same divine laws of charity for Muslims are indicated in the Noble Quran and The Prophet (PBUH)'s sayings. There is therefore a complete harmony between the signs of Allah (SWT) in nature, scientifically described by universal laws and His words in the Noble Quran. Moreover, after the gestures of charity perceived during the summer, autumn and winter, the reward is the beauty of the deserved spring. This reward of the Cyclic Flow of Charity is a sign that comes every year as a lesson for humanity. Indeed, similarly and according to the Noble Quran, helping people, animals and plants during our social and professional activities (muʿāmalāt) brings happiness and tranquility in our hearts as we self-purify our soul in the Eternal Path of Charity introduced in this book. Based on the Quran and the teaching of Prophet Muhammad (PBUH), this unseen Eternal Path of Charity could be related to The Straight Path as mentioned in the Quranic verse "And verily, [O Muhammad], are indeed guiding mankind to the Straight Path." (Quran; 42:52).

In the same way as we worship Allah (SWT) by practicing the five pillars of Islam (ibādāt), as Muslims we are also supposed to worship Him during our professional activities by helping people in workplaces (muʿāmalāt). Reactive helping (helping when asked) is recommended by the literature because the helpers perceived that they had a greater impact and fell more engaged at work. In this perspective, following the Islamic tradition, this book proposes the application of the two divine laws of charity in Muslim organizations in order to maximize the efficiency of the workflows and create a happy environment in workplaces. The most important is that employees at all levels of the organizations will be able to add their daily duties as good deeds in the Eternal Path of Charity.

Now, in contradiction with the divine laws of charity imposed by Allah (SWT) on the whole universe, in our societies based on consumerism, money flows from mostly poor consumers to the much richer companies and banks. Therefore, the increase of intensity of the natural disasters linked to global warming and the recent coronavirus pandemic could be warning signs from Allah (SWT) through nature in order to urge us to obey the divine laws of charity and change our lifestyle from consumerism to charity-based societies. Since education in key to solve social and technical problems the world is facing today, an Islam-based educational system is also proposed in this book in order to teach natural and social sciences under the umbrella of the Divine Science for the benefits of humanity with the Light of the Noble Quran and The Prophet (PBUH)'s sayings. The teaching methods of the Prophet (PBUH) will be the fundamental reference for all Muslim teachers to help students use fully their innate abilities and learn the corresponding skills and knowledge in order to be able to fulfill their divine duties in their future workplaces and add their daily activities as good deeds in the Eternal Path of Charity.

Reading the Noble Quran, I came to understand that it could also be an Eternal Path of Forgiveness. For example, the 2nd divine law of forgiveness could in this Quranic verse "Tell them, (O Prophet): "My servants who have committed excesses against themselves, do not despair of Allah's Mercy. Surely Allah forgives all sins. He is Most Forgiving, Most Merciful" (Quran; 39:53). On the other hand, the 1st divine law of forgiveness, which is the precondition of the 2nd law of forgiveness, could be in the following part of the verse "Turn to your Lord and surrender yourselves to Him before the chastisement over-takes you; for then you will receive no help" (Quran; 39:54). In conclusion, there is one Eternal Path of Charity related to our good deeds to please Allah (SWT) and one Eternal Path of Forgiveness for our bad deeds to obtain forgiveness from Him. The Day of Judgment is a Balance between the accepted good deeds and the unforgiven bad deeds. According to the Quranic verse "Wealth and children are an adornment of the life of the world. But the good righteous deeds that last are better for your Lord for rewards and better in respect of hope." (Quran; 18:46), we should not be happy or sad about the material things we have (finance, beauty and social position, children) because it is just a decoration and a test in this life. The most important is what we do with what Allah (SWT) provided us because only our actions and their intentions will be in the Balance of the Day of Judgment.

As mentioned in the Quranic verse "See, how We have exalted some above others in this world, and in the Life to Come they will have higher ranks and greater degrees of excellence over others" (Quran; 17:21), the Eternal reward in Paradise will be different for everyone depending on the result of the Balance.

Finally, it should be noted that no one will enter Paradise except by the mercy of Allah (SWT) as the Prophet said "Observe moderation (in doing deeds), and if you fail to observe it perfectly, try to do as much as you can do (to live up to this ideal of moderation) and be happy for none would be able to get into Paradise because of his deeds alone". They (the Companions of the Holy Prophet) said: Allah's Messenger, not even you? . Thereupon he said: "Not even me, but that Allah wraps me in His Mercy, and bear this in mind that the deed loved most by Allah is one which is done constantly even though it is small"[69].

"And who is fairer in speech than he who calls to Allah and acts righteously and says: I am a Muslim" (Quran: 41:33)

O Allah "The Responding One",

We beg You to make best our achievements, to make best our acts, to make best our deeds, and to make best our inside and our outside. We beg you to put us on the highest level in Paradise.

Ameen.

Abbreviation and Nomenclature

ABBREVIATIONS AND FULL MEANING

CS: Consumer Spending

CGPA: Cumulative Grade Point Average

COP: Conference of the Parties

DMF: Dadach Motivation Factor

FGP: Full Grade Point

GDP: Gross Domestic Product

IPCC: Intergovernmental Panel on Climate Change

KSA: Knowledge, Skills, Abilities

LPG: Liquefied Petroleum Gas

PBUH: Peace Be Upon Him

PE: Potential energy

SCL: Student-centered learning

FC: Social Flows for Consumption

SWT: "Subhanahu Wa Ta'ala" or "Glory to Him, the Exalted"

WFM: Work Force Management

NOMENCLATURE

A:	Surface area
E:	Energy
k:	Thermal conductivity
k_{air}:	Mass transfer coefficient of atmospheric air
P:	Pressure of atmospheric air
P_w:	Partial pressure of water
Q:	Heat
R:	Resistance
R_{air}:	Resistance of atmospheric air
T:	Temperature
t:	Time
WE:	Water exchanged per unit time during evaporation
WF:	Amount of rain or snow falling per unit time
WT:	Water exchanged per unit time during transportation

List of Tables and Figures

References

1.   Allah in Wikipedia

2.   Sahih Bukhari 50:894

3.   99 Names of Allah (Al Asma Ul Husna)
        https://99namesofallah.name/

4.   30 facts about Islam:
        https://www.30factsaboutislam.com/the-meaning-of-muslim/

5.   Ali, Shamsher. "Science and the Qur'an". In Oliver Leaman. The Qur'an: An Encyclopedia (PDF). p. 572. Retrieved13 May 2018.

6.   Muzaffar Iqbal (2007). Science & Islam. Greenwood Press.

7.   التطبيقات العملية والتقانية على الخلايا الكهروكيميائية

8.   التوصيل الحراري https://3lumalnawa.com/1440/03/04/heat-transfer-conduction/

9.   Sadullah Khan (2019), Stewardship of WATER, the Commodity of Life in Islamic City
        https://www.islamicity.org/7781/stewardship-of-water-the-commodity-of-life/?gclid=CjwKCAjwibzsBRAMEiwA1pHZrnRheLG

KY7ceb_ybqcN2kX5zAthv23WMYnT6V6NSsXG4FH
zR-VyTARoCLDAQAvD_BwE

10. رسومات-دورة-الماء-في-الطبيعة
https://www.pinterest.com/pin/276127020891499701/

11. Sunan al-Tirmidhī 2687

12. Nicholas Wade, (2009); We May Be Born With an Urge
to Help, Science, New York Times
https://www.nytimes.com/2009/12/01/science/01human.h
tml.

13. Sunan al-Tirmidhī 2517

14. ISLAMCITY: Zakat explained in
http://everything.explained.today/Zakat/

15. Fiqh-us-Sunnah, Volume 3, Number 98

16. Ṣaḥīḥ Muslim 2593

17. 40 Hadith Nawawi 13

18. Sahih al-Bukhari 2466

19. Ṣaḥīḥ al-Bukhārī 2195, Ṣaḥīḥ Muslim 1553

20. Business Dictionary.
http://www.businessdictionary.com/definition/organizatio
n.html

21.   Traci Moxson, (2014); THE RIGHT PEOPLE, IN THE RIGHT PLACE, AT THE RIGHT TIME; ICMI, Published: April 02, 2014.

22.   Ṣaḥīḥ al-Bukhārī 5665, Ṣaḥīḥ Muslim 2586

23.   When the Prophet migrated to Medina, how did he create religious coexistence? Dar Al Ifta El- Missriyyah. http://www.dar-alifta.org/Foreign/ViewArticle.aspx?ID=733&CategoryID=4

24.   Dr. Syadiyah Abdul Shukor (2019), Business Strategy and Strategic Planning From Islamic Perspective in ENTREPRENUERSHIP, ORGANISATIONAL BEHAVIOUR & ISLAMIC FOUNDATION, http://gsmuamalat.usim.edu.my/3141-2/

25.   Harrison Monarth (2016), Act Like a Leader: Help Others Succeed. Build Strategic Alliances. Know Yourself, in Entrepreneur https://www.entrepreneur.com/article/272725

26.   Shanna B. Tiayon (2019), When You Should Help Your Coworkers—and When to Think Twice; Greater Good wants to know: Do you think this article will influence your opinions or behavior?

https://greatergood.berkeley.edu/article/item/when_you_should_help_your_coworkers_and_when_to_think_twice

27.　At-Tirmidhi

28.　Sahih al-Bukhari, 8:73:56

29.　Sahih Muslim 2999

30.　Kendra Cherry, What Is Democratic Leadership? Characteristics, benefits, drawbacks, and famous examples, Verywell mind, October 23, 2018.

31.　Kendra Cherry, Autocratic Leadership: Key Characteristics, Strengths, and Weaknesses of Autocratic Leadership, Verywell mind, October 22, 2018.

32.　Braden Becker, The 7 Most Common Leadership Styles & How to Find Your Own, Hubspot, May 2018 https://blog.hubspot.com/marketing/leadership-styles.

33.　Sendjaya, Sen; Sarros, James C. (2002-09-01). "Servant Leadership: Its Origin, Development, and Application in Organizations". Journal of Leadership & Organizational Studies. 9 (2): 57–64. doi:10.1177/107179190200900205. ISSN 1548-0518.

34.　QURANREADING (2018): Top Leadership Qualities of the Holy Prophet Muhammad (PBUH): http://www.quranreading.com/blog/top-leadership-qualities-of-the-holy-prophet-muhammad-pbuh/

35.　Elizabeth Hopper, Helping Others Makes Better Leaders (5 Tips to Grow Others) in Approachable leadership. https://approachableleadership.com/helping-others/

36.　Kent Julian (2018); 10 Great Leadership Quotes for Helping Others Grow in Live it Forward.

https://liveitforward.com/10-great-leadership-quotes-for-helping-others-grow/

37. _Top Leadership Qualities of the Holy Prophet Muhammad (PBUH) (2015) in_ http://www.quranreading.com/blog/top-leadership-qualities-of-the-holy-prophet-muhammad-pbuh/

38. Mohsen Haredy, (2016); The Prophet's Wisdom in Leading His Companions in Islamic City https://www.islamicity.org/8607/the-prophets-wisdom-in-leading-his-companions.

39. Sahih Muslim, 91

40. Theresa Corbin, Muhammad (PBUH)- Prophet, Leader, Servant, 2017 https://aboutislam.net/reading-islam/about-muhammad/muhammad-pbuh-prophet-leader-servant/

41. Ṣaḥīḥ al-Bukhārī 6719, Ṣaḥīḥ Muslim 1829

42. Sahih Muslim 4487.

43. http://ncmh.org.sa/index.php/pages/psychologicalD/374

44. McLeod, S. A. (2018, May 21). Maslow's hierarchy of needs. Retrieved from https://www.simplypsychology.org/maslow.html.

45. Zin Eddine Dadach, 2021; The Utilization of a Universal Concept for the Modelisation of Consumer Spending,

Journal of Marketing Management and Consumer Behavior, Vol 3, No 2 (2021)

46.   Kimberly Amadeo, 2019, Consumer Spending Trends and Current Statistics in The Balance: https://www.thebalance.com/consumer-spending-trends-and-current-statistics-3305916

47.   Erin El Issa (2017); 2017 American Household Credit Card Debt Study in NERDWALLET'S https://www.nerdwallet.com/blog/credit-card-data/household-credit-card-debt-study-2017/

48.   Joshua Becker, 7 Ways to Sample Living With Less, becoming minimalist, https://www.becomingminimalist.com/minimalist-living/

49.   Theresa Domagalski and Tim Kasser (2002); The High Price of Materialism; The Academy of Management Review 29(1):135.

50.   Eric van Bemmel, Why feeling pain is key to our happiness, The University of Melbourne, 10 August 2017

51.   Quranic Definitions and Hadith Al-muflihûn, ridwân, Happiness in Islam, in Living Islam https://www.livingislam.org/k/qdh_e.htmlEric van Bemmel, Why feeling pain is key to our happiness, University of Melbourne, August 2017.

52. The Impact of Climate Change on Natural Disasters, Erath Observatory, 2017.

53. Andrea Thompson, Major Greenhouse Gas Reductions Needed by 2050: IPCC, Climate Central, April 13th, 2014.

54. Denise Chow, Carbon emissions dropped 17 percent globally amid coronavirus, NBC News, May 19, 2020, https://www.nbcnews.com/science/environment/carbon-emissions-dropped-17-percent-globally-amid-coronavirus-n1210331

55. Joachim Funke (2017), How Much Knowledge Is Necessary for Action? In Knowledge and Action pp 99-111, Springer.

56. Dr. Ragheb Elsergany (2011), Contributions of Muslims to the world in Islam story https://islamstory.com/index.php/en/artical/3407593

57. Ali, S. I. (2002). Sunnah of the Prophet: Educational Vision.: Dar Alfikr Al-Arabi.).

58. Vahap Gultekin (2012), The Educational Methods of Our Prophet (PBUH) in The Pen Magazine http://www.thepenmagazine.net/the-educational-methods-of-our-prophet-pbuh/

59. Kamal Shaarawy (2014), The Teaching Methods of the Prophet Muhammad (PBUH); The Message

International Magazine
https://messageinternational.org/the-teaching-methods-
of-the-prophet-muhammad-pbuh/

60.   Mihyar Hesson and Kaneez Fatima Shad (2007), A
        Student-Centered Learning Model, American Journal of
        Applied Sciences 4(9):628-636.

61.   Zin Eddine Dadach, 2013; Quantifying the effects of an
        active learning strategy on the motivation of students.
        International Journal of Engineering Education, Vol. 29,
        No. 4, pp. 904–913, 2013.

62.   Zin Eddine Dadach, 2016, "An introductory chemical
        engineering course based on analogies and research-based
        learning", International Journal of Engineering
        Education Vol. 32, No. 5(B), pp. 2194–2203, 2016.

63.   Sunan al-Tirmidhī 2685

64.   Sahih al-Bukhari 528

65.   Ṣaḥīḥ al-Bukhārī 6081, Ṣaḥīḥ Muslim 1051

67.   Sahih al-Bukhari 7498

68.   Sunan Abī Dāwūd 4681

69.   Ṣaḥīḥ al-Bukhārī 6099, Ṣaḥīḥ Muslim 281

www.ingramcontent.com/pod-product-compliance
Lightning Source LLC
Chambersburg PA
CBHW071155120626
46546CB00006B/2274